Cambridge Plain Texts

MONTAIGNE

FLORIO

T0346160

MONTAIGNE

FIVE ESSAYS

TRANSLATED BY

JOHN FLORIO

CAMBRIDGE
AT THE UNIVERSITY PRESS
1937

CAMBRIDGE UNIVERSITY PRESS
Cambridge, New York, Melbourne, Madrid, Cape Town,
Singapore, São Paulo, Delhi, Mexico City

Cambridge University Press
The Edinburgh Building, Cambridge CB2 8RU, UK

Published in the United States of America by Cambridge University Press, New York

www.cambridge.org
Information on this title: www.cambridge.org/9781107695160

© Cambridge University Press 1937

First Edition 1922
Reprinted 1932
,, 1937
First published 1937
Re-issued 2013

A catalogue record for this publication is available from the British Library

ISBN 978-1-107-69516-0 Paperback

NOTE

JOHN FLORIO (1553?–1625), reader in Italian to
Queen Anne, and dictionary-maker, rendered a
service to English literature which few translators have been so happy as to equal. Fortunate
both in time and in subject, he led the way into
that upper chamber in the tower of the château near
Bordeaux from whence Michel Eyquem, seigneur
de Montaigne (1533–1592) looked abroad over 'a
farre-extending, rich and unresisted prospect.' In
that famous panelled library, with a thousand
well-loved books around him, and with an intimate
knowledge of his own nature, Montaigne saw how
wonderfully *vain, divers, et ondoyant* is man, con-
structing a full-length portrait of himself, his pre-
ferences, his doubts, 'the very genius of quali-
fication' following 'him through all his keen, constant, changeful consideration of men and things.'
Montaigne's essays are '*un livre de bonne foi*';
their honesty and sincerity, their humanism, have,
from the first, influenced and captivated English
writers: even if the signature of Shakespeare on
a copy of Florio in the British Museum be an
eighteenth-century forgery, there appears to be
little doubt that Florio, as well as North, among
the Tudor translators, was familiar to Shakespeare; the signature of Ben Jonson on another
copy is probably genuine; Bacon and Cowley,
Sir William Temple and Halifax are in the direct
succession; to Edward FitzGerald, he was 'my
dear old Montaigne'; to Emerson, one of his

'Representative Men'; 'Montaigne and Howell's Letters,' says Thackeray, 'are my bedside books. If I wake at night, I have one or other of them to prattle me to sleep again. They talk about themselves for ever, and don't weary me' (*Roundabout Papers*); having Montaigne for its subject, chapter five, 'Suspended Judgment,' in Walter Pater's *Gaston de Latour* is one of the classics of interpretation.

Books One and Two of Montaigne's *Essays* were first published in 1580. Book Three was added in 1588 to a revised text of the earlier Books. The first edition of Florio's translation was published in 1603. He translated from more than one of the French editions, probably mainly from the posthumous edition of 1595, edited by Montaigne's *fille d'alliance* Mlle de Gournay and Pierre de Brach. The text of the five essays which follow is that of the third edition of Florio (1632).

It should be remembered that Montaigne not infrequently altered to suit his purpose the text of writers from whom he quoted.

A. R. W.

CAMBRIDGE,
10 *May*, 1922

CONTENTS

THE ESSAYES

OF

MICHAEL LORD OF MONTAIGNE

I. 1.

BY DIVERS MEANES MEN COME UNTO A LIKE END

THE most usuall way to appease those minds we have offended (when revenge lies in their hands, and that we stand at their mercy) is, by submission to move them to commiseration and pitty: Neverthelesse, courage, constancie, and resolution (meanes altogether opposite) have sometimes wrought the same effect. *Edward* the black Prince of *Wales* (who so long governed our Country of *Guienne*, a man whose conditions and fortune were accompanied with many notable parts of worth and magnanimitie) having beene grievously offended by the *Limosins*, though he by maine force tooke and entred their Citie, could by no meanes be appeased, nor by the wailefull out-cries of all sorts of people (as of men, women, and children) be moved to any pitty, they prostrating themselves to the common slaughter, crying for mercy, and humbly submitting themselves at his feet, untill such time as in triumphant manner passing thorow their Citie, he perceived three French Gentlemen, who alone, with an incredible and undaunted boldnesse, gainstood the enraged violence, and made head against the furie of his victorious armie. The consideration and respect of so notable a vertue, did first abate the dint of his wrath, and from those three began to relent, and shew mercy to all the other inhabitants of the said towne. *Scanderbeg*, Prince of *Epirus*, following one of his souldiers, with purpose to kill him, who by all means of humilitie, and submisse entreatie, had first assaied to pacifie him, in such an unavoidable extremitie, resolved at last, resolutely to encounter him with his sword in his hand. This resolution did immediately stay his Captains fury, who seeing him undertake so honourable an attempt, not only forgave, but received him into grace and favour. This example may haply, of such as have not knowne the prodigious force and matchlesse valour of the said Prince, admit another interpretation. The Emperour *Conradus*, third of that name, having besieged *Guelphe*, Duke of *Bavaria*, what vile or base satisfaction soever was offered him, would yeeld to no other milder conditions, but only to suffer such Gentlewomen as were with the Duke in the Citie (their honours safe) to issue out of the Towne afoot with such things as they could carry about them. They with an unrelenting courage advised and resolved themselves (neglecting all other riches or jewels) to carry their husbands, their children, and the Duke himselfe, on their backs: The Emperour perceiving the quaintnesse of their device, tooke so great pleasure at it, that hee wept for joy, and forthwith converted that former inexorable rage, and mortall hatred he bare the Duke, into so milde a relenting and gentle kindnesse, that thence forward he entreated both him and his with all favour and courtesie. Either of these wayes might easily perswade mee: for I am much inclined to mercie, and affected to mildnesse. So it is, that in mine opinion, I should more naturally

stoope unto compassion, than bend to estimation.
Yet is pitty held a vicious passion among the Stoicks.
They would have us aid the afflicted, but not to faint,
and co-suffer with them. These examples seeme fittest
for mee, forsomuch as these minds are seene to be
assaulted and environed by these two meanes, in un-
dauntedly suffering the one, and stooping under the
other. It may peradventure be said, that to yeeld ones
heart unto commiseration, is an effect of facility, ten-
dernesse, and meeknesse: whence it proceedeth, that
the weakest natures, as of women, children, and the
vulgar sort are more subject unto it. But (having
contemned teares and wailings) to yeeld unto the
onely reverence of the sacred Image of vertue, is the
effect of a couragious and imployable minde, holding
a masculine and constant vigour, in honour and affection. Notwithstanding, amazement and admiration
may in lesse generous minds worke the like effect.
Witnesse the Thebanes, who having accused and in-
dited their Captaines, as of a capitall crime, forsomuch
as they had continued their charge beyond the time
prescribed them, absolved and quit *Pelopidas* of all
punishment, because he submissively yeelded under
the burden of such objections, and to save himselfe,
imployed no other meanes, but suing-requests, and
demisse intreaties; where on the contrary, *Epaminon-
das* boldly relating the exploits achieved by him, and
with a fierce and arrogant manner upbraiding the
people with them, had not the heart so much as to
take their lots into his hands, but went his way, and
was freely absolved; the assembly much commending
the stoutnesse of his courage. *Dionysius* the elder,
after long-lingering and extreme difficulties, having

taken the Citie of *Reggio*, and in it the Captaine
Phyton (a worthy honest man) who had so obstinately
defended the same, would needs shew a tragicall
example of revenge. First, he told him, how the day
before, he had caused his sonne and all his kinsfolkes
to be drowned. To whom *Phyton*, stoutly out-staring
him, answered nothing, but that they were more happy
than himselfe by the space of one day. Afterward
he caused him to be stripped, and by his executioners
to be taken and dragged thorow the Citie most igno-
miniously, and cruelly whipping him, charging him
besides with outragious and contumelious speeches.
All which notwithstanding, as one no whit dismayed,
he ever shewed a constant and resolute heart; and
with a cheerfull and bold countenance went on still,
loudly recounting the honourable and glorious cause
of his death, which was, that he would never consent
to yeeld his Country into the hands of a cruell tyrant,
menacing him with an imminent punishment of the
Gods. *Dionysius* plainly reading in his Souldiers
lookes, that in lieu of animating them with braving
his conquered enemie, they in contempt of him, and
scorne of his triumph, seemed by the astonishment
of so rare a vertue, to be moved with compassion, and
inclined to mutinie, yea, and to free *Phyton* from out
the hands of his *Sergeants* or *Guard*, caused his torture
to cease, and secretly sent him to be drowned in the
sea. Surely, man is a wonderfull, vaine, divers, and
wavering subject: it is very hard to ground any
directly-constant and uniforme judgement upon him.
Behold *Pompey*, who freely pardoned all the Citie of
the *Mamertines*, (against which he was grievously enraged) for the love of the magnanimitie, and con-

sideration of the exceeding vertue of *Zeno*, one of their fellow-citizens, who tooke the publike fault wholly upon himselfe, and desired no other favour, but alone to beare the punishment thereof; whereas *Syllaes* host having used the like vertue in the Citie of *Perugia*, obtained nothing, neither for himselfe, nor for others. And directly against my first example, the hardiest amongst men, and so gracious to the vanquished, *Alexander* the great, after many strange difficulties, forcing the Citie of *Gaza*, encountred by chance with *Betis*, that commanded therein, of whose valour (during the siege) he had felt wonderfull and strange exploits, being then alone, forsaken of all his followers, his armes all-broken, all-besmeared with bloud and wounds, fighting amongst a number of Macedonians, who pell-mell laid still upon him; provoked by so deare a victorie, (for among other mishaps he had newly received two hurts in his body) said thus unto him; *Betis, thou shalt not die as thou wouldest: for make account thou must indure all the torments may possibly bee devised or inflicted upon a caitife wretch, as thou art.* But he, for all his enemies threats, without speaking one word, returned only an assured, sterne, and disdainefull countenance upon him; which silent obstinacie *Alexander* noting, said thus unto himselfe: *What? would hee not bend his knee? could he not utter one suppliant voyce? I will assuredly vanquish his silence, and if I cannot wrest a word from him, I will at least make him to sob or groane.* And converting his anger into rage, commanded his heeles to bee through-pierced, and so all alive with a cord through them, to be torne, mangled, and dismembred at a carts-taile. May it be, the force of his courage, was so naturall and peculiar unto him, that because he would no-whit admire him, he respected him the lesse? or deemed he it so proper unto himselfe, that in his height, he could not without the spight of envious passion, endure to see it in an other? or was the naturall violence of his rage incapable of any opposition? surely, had it received any restraint, it may be supposed, that in the ransacking and desolation of the Citie of *Thebes*, it should have felt the same; in seeing so many Worthies lost, and valiant men put to the sword, as having no meanes of publike defence; for above six thousand were slaine and massacred, of which not one was seene, either to run away, or beg for grace. But on the contrary, some here and there seeking to affront, and endeavouring to check their victorious enemies, urging and provoking them to force them die an honourable death. No one was seene to yeeld, and that to his last gaspe did not attempt to revenge himselfe, and with all weapons of dispaire, with the death of some enemie, comfort and sweeten his owne miserie. Yet could not the affliction of their vertue find any ruth or pitie, nor might one day suffice to glut or asswage his revengefull wrath. This butcherous slaughter continued unto the last drop of any remaining bloud; where none were spared but the unarmed and naked, the aged and impotent, the women and children; that so from amongst them, they might get thirtie thousand slaves.

I. 3.

OUR AFFECTIONS ARE TRANSPORTED BEYOND OUR SELVES

THOSE which still accuse men for ever gaping after future things, and go about to teach us, to take hold of present fortunes, and settle our selves upon them, as having no hold of that which is to come; yea much lesse than we have of that which is already past, touch and are ever harping upon the commonest humane error, if they dare call that an error, to which Nature her selfe, for the service of the continuation of her worke, doth addresse us, imprinting (as it doth many others) this false imagination in us, as more jealous of our actions, than of our knowledge. We are never in our selves, but beyond. Feare, desire, and hope, draw us ever towards that which is to come, and remove our sense and consideration from that which is, to amuse us on that which shall be, yea when we shall be no more. *Calamitosus est animus futuri anxius* (SEN. *Epi.* 98). *A minde in suspense what is to come, is in a pittifull case.*

This notable precept is often alleaged in *Plato. Follow thy businesse and know thy selfe*; Each of these two members, doth generally imply all our duty; and likewise enfolds his companion. He that should doe his businesse, might perceive that his first lesson is, to know what he is, and what is convenient for him. And he that knoweth himself, takes no more anothers matters for his owne, but above all other things, loveth and correcteth himself, rejecteth superfluous occupa-

tions, idle imaginations, and unprofitable propositions.
As if you grant follie what it desireth, it will no-whit
be satisfied; so is wisdome content with that which
is present, and never displeased with it selfe. *Epicurus*
doth dispense with his sage touching the foresight and
care of what shal insue. Amongst the lawes that regard
the deceased, that which ties the actions of Princes to
be examined when they are dead, seemes to me verie
solid. They are companions, if not masters of the
lawes: That which justice could not worke on their
heads, it is reason it effect upon their reputation, and
goods of their successors: things wee many times preferre before our lives. It is a custome brings many
singular commodities unto nations that observe it,
and to be desired of all good Princes: who have cause
to complaine that the memorie of the wicked is used
as theirs. Wee owe a like obedience and subjection
to all Kings; for it respects their office: but estimation
and affection, we owe it only to their vertue. If they
be unworthy, wee are to endure them patiently, to
conceale their vices, and to aid their indifferent actions
with our commendations, as long as their authoritie
hath need of our assistance, and that ought to be
ascribed unto politike order. But our commerce with
them being ended, there is no reason we should refuse
the unfolding of our felt wrongs unto justice and our
libertie. And specially to refuse good subjects, the
glory to have reverently and faithfully served a master,
whose imperfections were so well knowne unto them:
exempting posteritie from so profitable an example.
And such as for the respect of some private benefit
or interest, doe wickedly embrace the memorie of an
unworthy Prince, doe particular justice at the charge

of publike justice. *Titus Livius* speaketh truly, where he saith, that the speech of men brought up under a royaltie is ever full of vaine ostentations, and false witnesses; every man indifferently extolling the King, to the furthest straine of valour and soveraigne greatnesse. The magnanimitie of those two Souldiers may be reproved, one of which being demanded of *Nero*, why he hated him, answered him to his teeth; I loved thee whilest thou wast worthy of love, but since thou becamest a parricide, a fire-brand, a Juglar, a Player, and a Coach-man, I hate thee, as thou deservest. The other being asked, wherefore he sought to kill him, answered, Because I finde no other course to hinder thy uncessant outrages and impious deeds. But can any man, that hath his senses about him, justly reprove the publike and generall testimonies that since his death have beene given, and so shall be for ever, both against him and all such like reprobates, of his tyrannicall and wicked demeanours? I am sorrie that in so sacred a policie as the Lacedemonian was, so fained and fond a ceremonie at the death of their Kings was ever devised and brought in use. All their confederates and neighbours, all the slave-Helotes, men and women pell-mell, for a testimonie of their griefe and sorrow, did mangle and gash their foreheads, and in their out-cries and lamentations exclaimed, that their deceased King, howsoever he had lived, was and had beene the best Prince that ever they had, ascribing in order the commendations due unto desert, and to the last and latter ranke, what belongs unto the first merit. *Aristotle* that hath an oare in every water, and medleth with all things, makes a question about *Solons* speech, who saith, that no man

can truly be counted happy before his death. Whether
he that lived and died according to his wish, may be
named happy, whether his renowne be good or ill,
and whether his posteritie be miserable or no. Whilest
we stirre and remove, wee transport our selves by
preoccupation wheresoever wee list: but no sooner
are wee out of being, but wee have no communication
at all with that which is. And it were better to tell
Solon, that never man is happy then, since he never
is so, but when he is no more.

> *—Quisquam*
> *Vix radicitus è vita se tollit, et ejicit:*
> *Sed facit esse sui quiddam super inscius ipse,*
> *Nec removet satis à projecto corpore sese, et*
> *Vindicat.*—LUCR. *Rer. nat.* iii. 877.

Scarce any rids himselfe of life so cleere,
But leaves unwitting some part of him heere:
Nor frees or quits himselfe sufficiently
From that his body which forlorne doth lie.

Bertrand of *Gelsquin* died at the siege of the castle
of *Rancon*, neere unto *Puy* in *Avergne*: the besieged
yeelding afterward, were forced to carry the keies of
the Castle, upon the deceased body of the Captaine.
Bartholomew of *Alviano*, Generall of the Venetian
forces dying in their service and wars about *Brescia*,
and his bodie being to be transported to *Venice*,
through the territory of *Verona*, which then was
enemie unto them, the greatest part of the army
thought it expedient to demand a safe conduct for
their passage of those of *Verona*, to which *Theodoro
Trivulcio* stoutly opposed himselfe, and chose rather

to passe it by maine force, and to hazard the day, saying it was not convenient, that he who in his life time had never apprehended feare of his enemies should now being dead, seeme to feare them. Verily in like matters, by the lawes of *Greece*, hee that required a dead body of his enemies, with intent to bury the same, renounced the victory, and might no more erect any trophy of it: and he who was so required, purchased the title of honour and gaine. So did *Nicias* lose the advantage hee had clearely gained of the Corinthians; and contrariwise, *Agesilaus* assured that, hee doubtfully had gotten of the Bœotians. These actions might bee deemed strange, if in all ages it were not a common-received opinion, not only to extend the care of our selves, beyond this life, but also to beleeve, that heavenly favours doe often accompany us unto our grave, and continue in our posterity. Whereof there are so many examples (leaving our moderne a part) that I need not wade farre into it.

Edward the first King of *England*, in the long wars he had with *Robert* King of *Scotland*, having by triall found how greatly his presence advantaged the successe of his affaires, and how he was ever victorious in any enterprise he undertooke in his owne person; when hee died, bound his sonne by solemne oath, that being dead he should cause his body to be boyled, untill the flesh fell from the bones, which he should cause to be interred, and carefully keeping the bones, ever carry them about him, whensoever hee should happen to have wars with the Scots: As if destiny had fatally annexed the victory unto his limmes. *John Zisca*, who for the defence of *Wickliffs* opinions so much troubled the state of *Bohemia*, commanded

that after his death his body should be flead, and a
drum made of his skin, to be carried and sounded
in all the wars against his enemies: deeming the sound
of it would be a meanes to continue the advantages,
which in his former warres hee had obtained of them.
Certaine Indians did likewise carry the bones of one
of their Captaines in the skirmishes they had with the
Spaniards, in regard of the good successe hee had,
whilest hee lived, against them: And other nations of
that new-found world, doe likewise carry the bodies
of such worthy and fortunate men with them, as have
died in their battels, to serve them in stead of good
fortune and encouragement. The first examples re-
serve nothing else in their tombes, but the reputation
acquired by their former atchievements: but these
will also adjoyne unto it the power of working. The
act of Captaine *Bayart* is of better composition, who
perceiving himselfe deadly wounded by a shot received in his body, being by his men perswaded to
come off and retire himselfe from out the throng,
answered, he would not now so neere his end, begin
to turn his face from his enemie: and having stoutly
foughten so long as he could stand, feeling himselfe to
faint and stagger from his horse, commanded his
steward to lay him against a tree, but in such sort,
that he might die with his face toward the enemie;
as indeed hee did. I may not omit this other example,
as remarkable for this consideration, as any of the
precedent. The Emperour *Maximilian*, great grand-
father to *Philip* now King of *Spaine*, was a Prince highly
endowed with many noble qualities, and amongst
others with a well-nigh matchlesse beauty and comelinesse of body; but with other customes of his, hee

had this one much contrarie to other Princes, who to
dispatch their weightiest affaires make often their
close stoole, their regall Throne or Councel-chamber,
which was, that hee would not permit any groome
of his chamber (were hee never so neere about him)
to see him in his inner chamber...The instruction
which *Cyrus* giveth his children, that neither they nor
any other should either see or touch his body, after
the breath were once out of it; I ascribe it unto some
motive of devotion in him. For both his historian and
himselfe, amongst many other notable qualities they
are endued with, have throughout all the course of
their life seemed to have a singular respect and awfull
reverence unto religion. That story displeased mee
very much, which a nobleman told me of a kinsman
of mine (a man very famous and well known both in
peace and warre) which is, that dying very aged in
his court, being much tormented with extreme pangs
of the stone, hee with an earnest and unwearied care,
employed all his last houres, to dispose the honour
and ceremony of his funerals, and summoned all the
nobilitie that came to visit him, to give him assured
promise to be as assistants, and to convey him to his
last resting place. To the very same Prince, who was
with him at his last gasp, he made very earnest suit,
he would command all his houshold to wait upon him
at his interment, inforcing many reasons, and alleaging
divers examples, to prove that it was a thing very
convenient, and fitting a man of his qualitie: which
assured promise when he had obtained, and had at
his pleasure marshalled the order how they should
march, he seemed quietly and contentedly to yeeld
up the ghost. I have seldome seene a vanitie continue

so long. This other curiositie meere opposite unto it
(which to prove I need not labour for home-examples)
seemeth in my opinion cosen-german to this, that is,
when one is ever ready to breathe his last, carefully
and passionately to endevour how to reduce the con-
voy of his obsequies unto some particular and un-
wonted parcimonie, to one servant and to one lanterne.
I heare the humour and appointment of *Marcus
Æmilius Lepidus* commended, who expressly forbade
his heires to use those ceremonies about his interment,
which in such cases were formerly accustomed. Is it
temperance and frugalitie, to avoid charge and voluptuousnesse, the use and knowledge of which is
imperceptable unto us? Loe here an easie reformation,
and of small cost. Were it requisite to appoint any,
I would be of opinion, that as well in that, as in all
other actions of mans life, every man should referre
the rule of it to the qualitie of his fortune. And the
Philosopher *Lycon* did wisely appoint his friends to
place his body where they should thinke it fittest and
for the best: and for his obsequies, they should
neither be superfluous and over-costly, nor base and
sparing. For my part, I would wholly relie on custome, which should dispose this ceremonie, and would
yeeld my selfe to the discretion of the first or next
into whose hands I might chance to fall. *Totus hic
locus est contemnendus in nobis, non negligendus in
nostris: All this matter should be despised of us, but not
neglected of ours.* And religiously said a holy man;
*Curatio funeris, conditio sepulturæ, pompa exequiarum,
magis sunt vivorum solatia, quàm subsidia mortuorum*
(AUG. *Civ. Dei*, i. 12, verb. apost. ser. 32). *The pro-
curation of funerals, the maner of buriall, the pomp of*

*obsequies, are rather comforts to the living, than helps
to the dead.* Therefore *Socrates* answered *Criton*, who
at the houre of his death asked him how he would be
buried: *Even as you please*, said he. Were I to meddle
further with this subject, I would deeme it more
gallant to imitate those who yet living and breathing,
undertake to enjoy the order and honour of their
sepulchres, and that please themselves to behold their
dead countenance in Marble. Happy they that can
rejoyce and gratifie their senses with insensibilitie, and
live by their death! A little thing would make me
conceive an inexpiable hatred against all popular
domination; although it seeme most naturall and just
unto me; when I call to minde that inhumane in-
justice of the Athenians, who without further triall
or remission, yea without suffering them so much as
to reply or answer for themselves, condemned those
noble and worthy Captaines, that returned victoriously
from the sea-battell, which they (neere the Iles
Arginusæ) had gained of the Lacedemonians; the most
contested, bloodie and greatest fight the Grecians ever
obtained by sea with their owne forces: forsomuch as
after the victory, they had rather followed those
occasions, which the law of warre presented unto them,
for their availe, than to their prejudice staid to gather
and bury their dead men. And the successe of *Dio-
medon* makes their ruthlesse execution more hatefull,
who being a man of notable and exemplar vertue,
both military and politike, and of them so cruelly
condemned; after he had heard the bloudy sentence,
advancing himselfe forward to speake, having fit
opportunitie and plausible audience; he, I say, in
stead of excusing himselfe, or endevouring to justifie

his cause, or to exasperate the evident iniquity of so cruell a doome, expressed but a care of the Judges preservation, earnestly beseeching the Gods to turne that judgement to their good, praying that for want of not satisfying the vowes which hee and his companions had vowed in acknowledgement and thanksgiving for so famous a victory, and honourable fortune, they might not draw the wrath and revenge of the Gods upon them, declaring what their vowes were. And without more words, or urging further reasons, couragiously addressed himselfe to his execution. But fortune some yeares after punished him alike, and made him taste of the verie same sauce. For *Chabrias*, Captaine Generall of their sea-fleet, having afterward obtained a famous victory of *Pollis*, Admirall of *Sparta*, in the Ile of *Naxos*, lost absolutely the benefit of it, and onely contented with the day (a matter of great consequence for their affaires) fearing to incurre the mischiefe of this example, and to save a few dead carcasses of his friends, that floated up and downe the sea, gave leasure to an infinite number of his living enemies, whom he might easily have surprized to saile away in safety, who afterward made them to purchase their importunate superstition, at a deere-deere rate.

> *Quæris, quo jaceas, post obitum, loco?*
> *Quo non nata jacent.*—SEN. *Troas.* chor. ii. 30.

> Where shall you lie when you are dead?
> Where they lye that were never bred:

This other restores the sense of rest unto a body without a soule.

Neque sepulchrum, quo recipiat, habeat portum corporis.
Ubi remissa humana vita, corpus requiescat à malis.
                                    CIC. *Tusc. Qu.* i. Enni.

To turne in as a hav'n, have he no grave,
Where life left, from all griefe he rest may have.

Even as Nature makes us to see, that many dead
things have yet certaine secret relations unto life.
Wine doth alter and change in sellers, according to
the changes and alterations of the seasons of its vine-
yard. And the flesh of wilde beasts and venison doth
change qualitie and taste in the powdering-tubs,
according to the nature of living flesh, as some say
that have observed it.

II. 6.

OF EXERCISE OR PRACTICE

It is a hard matter (although our conceit doe willingly apply it selfe unto it) that Discourse and Instruction, should sufficiently be powerful, to direct us to action, and addresse us to performance, if over and besides that, we doe not by experience exercise and frame our minde, to the traine whereunto we will range it: otherwise, when we shall be on the point of the effects, it will doubtlesse finde it selfe much engaged and empeached. And that is the reason why amongst Philosophers, those that have willed to attaine to some greater excellence, have not beene content, at home, and at rest to expect the rigors of fortune, for feare she should surprise them unexperienced and finde them novices, if she should chance to enter fight with them; but have rather gone to meet and front her before, and witting-earnestly cast themselves to the triall of the hardest difficulties. Some have thereby voluntarily forsaken great riches, onely to practise a voluntarie povertie: others have willingly found out labour, and an austeritie of a toylesome life, thereby to harden and enure themselves to evill, and travell: othersome have frankly deprived themselves of the dearest and best parts of their body, as of their eyes, and members of generation, lest their over-pleasing, and too-too wanton service, might in any sort mollifie and distract the constant resolution of their minde. But to dye, which is the greatest worke we have to doe, exercise can nothing availe us thereunto. A man may, by custome and experience, fortifie himselfe against

griefe, sorrow, shame, want, and such like accidents:
But concerning death, we can but once feele and trie
the same. We are all novices, and new to learne when
we come unto it. There have, in former times, beene
found men so good husbands and thrifty of time, that
even in death they have assayed to taste and savour it;
and bent their minde to observe and see, what manner
of thing that passage of death was; but none did ever
yet come backe againe to tell us tidings of it.

> —*nemo expergitus extat*
> *Frigida quem semel est vitai pausa sequuta.*
> LUCR. iii. 929.

No man doth ever-after wake,
Whom once his lifes cold rest doth take.

Canius Julius, a noble Romane, a man of singular
vertue and constancie, having beene condemned to
death by that lewdly-mischievous monster of men,
Caligula: besides many marvelous evident assurances
he gave of his matchlesse resolution, when he was
even in the nicke to endure the last stroke of the
executioner; a Philosopher, being his friend, interrupted him with this question, saying: *Canius*, in what
state is your soule now; what doth she; what thoughts
possesse you now? I thought (answered he) to keepe
me ready and prepared with all my force, to see whether
in this instant of death, so short and so neere at hand,
I might perceive some dislodging or distraction of the
soule, and whether it will shew some feeling of her
sudden departure; that (if I apprehend or learne any
thing of her) I may afterward, if I can, returne, and
give advertisement thereof unto my friends. Loe-here
a Philosopher, not only untill death, but even in death

it selfe: what assurance was it, and what fierceness of courage, to will that his owne death should serve him as a lesson, and have leasure to thinke else where in a matter of such consequence;

—*jus hoc animi morientis habebat.*
LUCAN, viii. 636.

This power of minde had he,
When it from him did flee.

Me seemeth neverthelesse, that in some sort there is a meane to familiarize our selves with it, and to assay it. We may have some experience of it, if not whole and perfect, at least such as may not altogether be unprofitable, and which may yeelde us better fortified and more assured. If we cannot attaine unto it, we may at least approch it, and discerne the same: And if we cannot enter her fort, yet shal we see and frequent the approches unto it. It is not without reason we are taught to take notice of our sleepe, for the resemblance it hath with death. How easily we passe from waking to sleeping; with how little interest we lose the knowledge of light, and of our selves. The facultie of sleepe might haply seeme unprofitable, and against nature, sithence it depriveth us of all actions, and barreth us of all sense, were it not that nature doth thereby instruct us, that she hath equally made us, as well to live, as to die; and by life presenteth the eternal state unto us, which she after the same reserveth for us, so to accustome us thereunto, and remove the feare of it from us. But such as by some violent accident are falne into a faintnes of heart, and have lost all senses, they, in mine opinion, have well-nigh beene, where they might behold her true and

naturall visage: For, touching the instant or moment
of the passage, it is not to be feared, it should bring
any travell or displeasure with it, forasmuch as we
can have, nor sense, nor feeling without leasure. Our
sufferances have need of time, which is so short, and
plunged in death, that necessarily it must be insensible.
It is the approches that lead unto it we should feare;
and those may fall within the compasse of mans experience. Many things seeme greater by imagination,
than by effect. I have passed over a good part of my
age in sound and perfect health. I say, not only sound,
but blithe and wantonly-lustfull. That state full of
lust, of prime and mirth, made me deeme the consideration of sicknesses so yrkesome and horrible,
that when I came to the experience of them, I have
found their fits but weake, and their assaults but faint,
in respect of my apprehended feare. Lo here what I
daily prove. Let me be under a roofe, in a good chamber, warme-clad, and well at ease in some tempestuous
and stormy night. I am exceedingly perplexed, and
much grieved for such as are abroad, and have no
shelter: But let me be in the storme my selfe, I doe
not so much as desire to be elsewhere. Only to be
continually pent up in a chamber, seemed intolerable
to me. I have now enured my selfe to live a whole
weeke, yea a moneth in my chamber full of care,
trouble, alteration and weaknesse; and have found,
that in the time of my best health I moaned such as
were sicke, much more than I can well moane my
selfe when I am ill at ease: and that the power of my
apprehension did well-nigh halfe endeare the essence
and truth of the thing it selfe. I am in good hope the
like will happen to me of death: and that it is not

worth the labour I take for so many preparations as
I prepare against her: and so many helpes as I call
to sustaine, and assemble to endure the shocke and
violence of it. But hab or nab we can never take too
much advantage of it. During our second or third
troubles (I doe not well remember which) I fortuned
one day, for recreation sake, to goe forth and take the
ayre, about a league from my house, who am seated
even in the bowels of all troubles of our civill warres
of *France*, supposing to be most safe, so neere mine
owne home and retreite, that I had no need of better
attendance or equipage. I was mounted upon a very
easie-going nag, but not very sure. At my returning
home againe, a sudden occasion being offered me, to
make use of this nag in a peece of service, whereto he
was neither trained nor accustomed, one of my men
(a strong sturdy fellow) mounted upon a young strong-
headed horse, and that had a desperate hard mouth,
fresh, lusty and in breath; to shew his courage, and to
out-goe his fellowes, fortuned with might and maine
to set spurres unto him, and giving him the bridle,
to come right into the path where I was, and as a
Colossus with his weight riding over me and my nag,
that were both very little, he overthrew us both, and
made us fall with our heeles upward: so that the nag
lay along astonied in one place, and I in a trance
groveling on the ground ten or twelfe paces wide of
him; my face all torne and brused, my sword which
I had in my hand a good way from me, my girdle
broken, with no more motion or sense in me than
a stocke. It is the only swowning that ever I felt yet.
Those that were with me, after they had assayed all
possible meanes to bring me to my selfe again, sup-

posing me dead, tooke me in their armes, and with
much adoe were carying me home to my house, which
was about halfe a french league thence: upon the
way, and after I had for two houres space, by all,
beene supposed dead and past all recoverie, I began
to stir and breathe; for, so great aboundance of bloud
was falne into my stomake, that to discharge it, nature
was forced to rowze up her spirits. I was immediately
set upon my feet, and bending forward, I presently
cast up, in quantitie as much clottie pure bloud, as
a bucket will hold, and by the way was constrained
to doe the like divers times before I could get home,
whereby I began to recover a little life, but it was by
little and little, and so long adoing, that my chiefe
senses were much more enclining to death than to life.

> *Perche dubbiosa ancor del suo ritorno*
> *Non s'assicuta attonita la mente.*

> For yet the minde doubtfull it's returne
> Is not assured, but astonished.

The remembrance whereof (which yet I beare
deeply imprinted in my minde) representing me her
visage and *Idea* so lively and so naturally, doth in some
sort reconcile me unto her. And when I began to see,
it was with so dim, so weake and so troubled a sight,
that I could not discerne anything of the light.

> —*come quel ch'or apre, or chiude*
> *Gli occhi, mezzo tra'l sonno è l' esser desto.*

> As he that sometimes opens, sometimes shuts
> His eyes, betweene sleepe and awake.

Touching the function of the soule, they started up
and came in the same progresse as those of the body.

I perceived my selfe all bloudy; for my doublet was all sullied with the bloud I had cast. The first conceit I apprehended, was, that I had received some shot in my head; and in truth, at the same instant, there were divers that shot round about us. Me thought, my selfe had no other hold of me, but of my lips-ends. I closed mine eyes, to helpe (as me seemed) to send it forth, and tooke a kinde of pleasure to linger and languishingly to let my selfe goe from my selfe. It was an imagination swimming superficially in my minde, as weake and as tender as all the rest: but in truth, not only exempted from displeasure, but rather commixt with that pleasant sweetnesse, which they feele that suffer themselves to fall into a soft-slumbring and sense-entrancing sleepe. I beleeve it is the same state, they find themselves in, whom in the agony of death we see to droop and faint thorow weaknesse: and am of opinion, we plaine and moane them without cause, esteeming that either they are agitated with grievous pangs, or that their soule is pressed with painfull cogitations. It was ever my conceit, against the opinion of many, yea and against that of *Stephanus la Boetie*, that those whom we see, so over-whelmed, and faintly-drooping at the approches of their end, or utterly cast downe with the lingring tediousnesse of their deseases, or by accident of some apoplexie, or falling-evill,

—(*vi morbi sæpe coactus*
Ante oculos aliquis nostros ut fulminis ictu,
Concidit, et spumas agit, ingemit, et fremit artus,
Desipit, extentat nervos, torquetur, anhelat,
Inconstanter et in jactando membra fatigat).
Lucr. iii. 487.

(Some man by force of sicknesse driv'n doth fall,
As if by thunder stroke, before our eyes;
He fomes, he grones, he trembles over all,
He raves, he stretches, he's vext, panting lyes,
He tyr's his limmes by tossing,
Now this now that way crossing.)

or hurt in the head, whom we heare throb and rattle,
and send forth grones and gaspes, although we gather
some tokens from them, whereby it seemeth, they
have yet some knowledge left and certaine motions
we see them make with their body: I say, I have ever
thought, they had their soule and body buried and
asleepe.

Vivit et est vitæ nescius ipse suæ.
OVID, *Trist.* i. *El.* iii. 12.

He lives yet knowes not he,
That he alive should be.

And I could not beleeve, that at so great an astonishment of members, and deffailance of senses, the soule
could maintaine any force within, to know herselfe;
and therefore had no manner of discourse tormenting
them, which might make them judge and feele the
misery of their condition, and that consequently they
were not greatly to be moaned. As for my selfe,
I imagine no state so intolerable nor condition so
horrible, as to have a feelingly-afflicted soule, void
of meanes to disburthen and declare her selfe: As I
would say of those we send to execution, having first
caused their tongue to be cut out were it not that in
this manner of death, the most dumbe seemes unto
me the fittest, namely, if it be accompanied with a
resolute and grave countenance. And as those

miserable prisoners which light in the hands of those hard-harted and villenous Souldiers of these times, of whom they are tormented with all maner of cruell entreatie, by compulsion to drawe them unto some excessive and unpossible ransome, keeping them al that while in so hard a condition and place, that they have no way left them to utter their thoughts and expresse their miserie. The Poets have fained, there were some Gods, that favoured the release of such as sufferd so languishing deaths.

> —*hunc ego Diti*
> *Sacrum jussa fero, teque isto corpore solvo.*
> Virg. *Æn.* iv. 703, Iris.

> This to death sacred, I, as was my charge,
> Doe beare, and from this body thee enlarge.

And the faltering speeches and uncertaine answers, that by continuall ringing in their eares and incessant urging them, are somtimes by force wrested from them or by the motions which seeme to have some simpathy with that whereof they are examined, is notwithstanding no witnes that they live at least a perfect sound life. We do also in yawning, before sleep fully seize upon us, apprehend as it were in a slumber, what is done about us, and with a troubled and uncertaine hearing, follow the voyces, which seeme to sound but on the outward limits of our soule; and frame answers according to the last words we heard, which taste more of chance than of sense: which thing now I have proved by experience, I make no doubt, but hitherto, I have well judged of it. For, first lying as in a trance, I laboured even with my nailes to open my doublet (for I was unarmed) and well I wot, that in my imagination I felt nothing did hurt me. For, there are severall motions in us, which proceed not of our free wil.

Semianimesque micant digiti, ferrumque retractant.
x. 396.

> The halfe-dead fingers stirre, and feele,
> (Though it they cannot stirre) for steele.

Those that fall, doe commonly by a naturall impulsion cast their armes abroad before their falling, which sheweth, that our members have certaine offices, which they lend one to another, and possesse certaine agitations, apart from our discourse:

Falciferos memorant currus abscindere membra,
Ut tremere in terra videatur ab artubus, id quod
Decidit abscissum, cùm mens tamen atque hominis vis
Mobilitate mali non quit sentire dolorem.
LUCR. iii. 642.

They say, sith-bearing chariots limbes bereave,
So as on earth, that which cut-off they leave,
Doth seeme to quake; when yet mans force and minde
Doth not the paine, through so quick motion, finde.

My stomacke was surcharged with clotted bloud, my hands of themselves were still running to it, as often they are wont (yea against the knowledge of our will) where we feele it to itch. There are many creatures, yea and some men, in whom after they are dead, we may see their muskles to close and stirre. All men know by experience, there be some parts of our bodies, which often without any consent of ours doe stirre, stand and lye downe againe. Now these passions, which but exteriourly touch us, cannot properly be termed ours; For, to make them ours, a man must wholy be engaged unto them: And the paines that our feet or hands feele whilst we sleepe, are not ours. When I came neere my house, where the tidings of my fall was already come, and those of my houshold met me, with such outcries as are used in like times, I did not only answer some words, to what I was demanded, but some tell me, I had the memory to command my men to give my wife a horse, whom I perceived to be over-tired, and labouring in the way, which is very hilly, foule, and rugged. It seemeth this consideration proceeded from a vigilant soule: yet was I cleane distracted from it, they were but vaine conceits, and as in a cloud, only moved by the sense of the eyes and eares: They came not from my selfe. All which notwithstanding, I knew neither whence I came, nor whither I went, nor could I understand or consider what was spoken unto me. They were but light effects, that my senses produced of themselves, as it were of custome. Whatsoever the soule did assist it with, was but a dreame, being lightly touched, and only sprinkled by the soft impression of the senses. In the meane time my state was verily most pleasant and easefull. I felt no manner of care or affliction, neither for my selfe nor others. It was a slumbering, languishing and extreme weaknesse, without any paine at all. I saw mine owne house and knew it not; when I was laid in my bed, I felt great ease in my rest, For I had beene vilely hurred and haled by those poore men, which had taken the paines to carry me upon their armes a long and wearysome way, and to say truth, they had all beene wearied twice or thrice over, and were faine to shift severall times.

Many remedies were presently offered me, but I tooke none, supposing verily I had beene deadly hurt in the head. To say truth, it had beene a very happy death: For, the weaknesse of my discourse hinderd me from judging of it, and the feeblenesse of my body from feeling the same. Me thought I was yeelding up the ghost so gently, and after so easie and indolent a manner, that I feele no other action lesse burthensome than that was. But when I began to come to life againe and recover my former strength,

> *Ut tandem sensus convaluere mei*,
> OVID, *Trist*. i. *El*. iii. 14.

At last when all the sprites I beare,
Recall'd and recollected were,

which was within two or three houres after, I presently felt my selfe full of aches and paines all my body over; for, each part thereof was with the violence of the fall much brused and tainted; and for two or three nights after I found my self so ill, that I verily supposed I shold have had another fit of death: But that a more lively, and sensible one: (and to speak plaine) I feele my bruses yet, and feare me shall do while I live: I will not forget to tell you, that the last thing I could rightly fall into againe, was the remembrance of this accident, and I made my men many times to repeat me over and over againe, whither I was going, whence I came, and at what houre that chance befell me, before I could throughly conceive it. Concerning the manner of my falling, they in favour of him who had beene the cause of it, concealed the truth from me, and told me other flim flam tales. But a while after, and the morrow next when my memorie began to come to it

selfe againe, and represent the state unto me, wherein
I was at the instant, when I perceived the horse riding
over me (for being at my heeles, I chanced to espy
him, and helde my selfe for dead; yet was the conceit
so sudden, that feare had no leasure to enter my
thoughts) me seemed it was a flashing or lightning,
that smote my soule with shaking, and that I came
from another world. This discourse of so slight an
accident, is but vaine and frivolous, were not the
instructions I have drawne from thence for my use:
For truly, for a man to acquaint himselfe with death,
I finde no better way than to approch unto it. Now
as *Plinie* saith, every man is a good discipline unto
himselfe, alwayes provided he be able to prie into
himself. This is not my doctrine, it is but my study;
And not another mans lesson, but mine owne; Yet
ought no man to blame me if I impart the same.
What serves my turne, may haply serve another mans;
otherwise I marre nothing; what I make use of, is
mine owne; And if I play the foole, it is at mine owne
cost, and without any other bodies interest. For it is
but a kind of folly, that dyes in me, and hath no traine.
We have notice but of two or three former ancients,
that have trodden this path; yet can we not say,
whether altogether like unto this of mine, for we know
but their names. No man since hath followed their
steps: it is a thorny and crabbed enterprise, and more
than it makes shew of, to follow so strange and vaga-
bond a path, as that of our spirit: to penetrate the
shady, and enter the thicke-covered depths of these
internall winding crankes; To chuse so many, and
settle so severall aires of his agitations: And tis a new
extraordinary ammusing, that distracts us from the

common occupation of the world, yea and from the most recommended: Many yeares are past since I have no other aime, whereto my thoughts bend, but my selfe, and that I controule and study nothing but my selfe. And if I study any thing else, it is immediatly to place it upon, or to say better, in my selfe. And me thinkes I erre not, as commonly men doe in other sciences, without all comparison lesse profitable. I impart what I have learn't by this, although I greatly content not my selfe with the progress I have made therein. *There is no description so hard, nor so profitable, as is the description of a mans owne life*; Yet must a man handsomely trimme-up, yea and dispose and range himself to appeare on the Theatre of this world. Now I continually tricke up my selfe; for I uncessantly describe my selfe. Custome hath made a mans speech of himselfe vicious. And obstinately forbids it in hatred of boasting, which ever seemeth closely to follow ones selfe witnesses, whereas a man should wipe a childes nose, that is now called to un-nose himselfe.

> *In vicium ducit culpæ fuga.*
> HOR. *Art. Poet.* 31.

> Some shunning of some sinne,
> Doe draw some further in.

I finde more evill than good by this remedy: But suppose it were true, that for a man to entertaine the company with talking of himselfe, were necessarily presumption: I ought not following my generall intent, to refuse an action that publisheth this crazed quality, since I have it in my selfe: and I should not conceale this fault, which I have not only in use, but in profession. Nevertheless to speake my opinion of it, this custome to condemne wine is much to blame, because many are therewith made drunke. Only good things may be abused. And I beleeve this rule hath only regard to popular defects: They are snaffles wherewith neither Saints, nor Philosophers, nor Divines, whom we heare so gloriously to speake of themselves, will in any sort be bridled. No more doe I, though I be no more the one than other. If they write purposely or directly of it, yet when occasion doth conveniently leade them unto it, faine they not, headlong to cast themselves into the lists? Whereof doth *Socrates* treat more at large, than of himselfe? To what doth he more often direct his Disciples discourses, than to speake of themselves, not for their bookes lesson, but of the essence and moving of their soule? We religiously shrive our selves to God and our Confessor, as our neighbours to all the people. But will some answer me, we report but accusation; wee then report all: For, even our vertue it selfe is faulty and repentable; My art and profession, is to live. Who forbids me to speake of it, according to my sense, experience, and custome; Let him appoint the Architect to speake of buildings, not according to himselfe, but his neighbours, according to anothers skill, and not his owne. If it be a glory, for a man to publish his owne worth himselfe, why doth not *Cicero* prefer the eloquence of *Hortensius*, and *Hortensius* that of *Cicero*? Some may peradventure suppose that by deeds and effects, and not simply by words, I witnesse of my selfe. I principally set forth my cogitations; a shapelesse subject, and which cannot fall within the compasse of a worke-manlike production;

with much adoe can I set it downe in this ayrie body
of the voice. Wiser men, and more learned and devout,
have lived avoiding all apparent effects. Effects would
speake more of fortune, than of me. They witnesse
their part, and not mine; unlesse it be conjecturally
and uncertainly: Parcels of a particular shew: I wholy
set forth and expose my selfe: It is a *Sceletos*: where
at first sight appeare all the vaines, muskles, gristles,
sinnewes, and tendons, each severall part in his due
place. The effect of the cough produceth one part,
that of palenesse or panting of the heart another, and
that doubtfully. I write not my gests, but my selfe and
my essence. I am of opinion that a man must be very
wise to esteeme himselfe, and equally consciencious
to give testimony of it: be it low, be it high indifferently.
If I did absolutely seeme good and wise unto myselfe,
I would boldly declare it. To speake lesse of himselfe
than he possesseth, is folly and not modesty. To pay
himselfe for lesse than he is worth, is basenesse and
pusilanimity, saith *Aristotle*. No vertue aids it selfe
with false-hood; and truth is never a matter of errour.
And yet for a man to say more of him selfe, than he
can well prove, is not ever presumption, though often
sottishnesse. For a man to over-weene, and please
himselfe exceedingly with what he is, and fall into
indiscreet love with himselfe, is in my conceit, the
substance of this vice. The best remedy to cure him,
is to doe cleane contrary to that which those appoint,
who in forbidding men to speake of themselves, doe
consequently also inhibit more to thinke of themselves. *Pride consisteth in conceit*: The tongue can have
no great share in it. For one to ammuse on himselfe,
is in their imagination to please himselfe: And for

a man to frequent and practise himselfe, is at an over-deare rate to please himselfe. But this excesse doth only breed in them, that but superficially feele and search themselves, that are seene to follow their affaires, which call idlenesse and fondnesse, for a man to entertaine, to applaud and to endeare himselfe, and frame Chimeraes, or build Castles in the ayre; deeming themselves as a third person and strangers to themselves. If any be besotted with his owne knowledge, looking upon himselfe, let him cast his eyes towards former ages, his pride shall be abated, his ambition shall be quailed; for there shall he finde many thousands of spirits, that will cleane suppresse and tread him under. If he fortune to enter into any selfe-presumption of his owne worth, let him but call to remembrance the lives of *Scipio* and *Epaminon-das*; so many armies, and so many Nations, which leave him so far behind them. No particular quality shall make him proud, that therewith shall reckon so many imperfect and weake qualities that are in him, and at last the nullity of humane condition. Forso-much as *Socrates* had truly only nibled on the precept of his God, to know himselfe, and by that study had learned to contemne himselfe, he alone was esteemed worthy of the name of Wise. Whosoever shall so know himselfe, let him boldly make himselfe knowne by his owne mouth.

II. 10.

OF BOOKES

I MAKE no doubt but it shall often befall me to speake of things, which are better, and with more truth handled by such as are their crafts-masters. Here is simply an Essay of my naturall faculties, and no whit of those I have acquired. And he that shall tax me with ignorance, shall have no great victory at my hands; for hardly could I give others reason for my discourses, that give none unto my selfe, and am not well satisfied with them. He that shall make search after knowledge, let him seeke it where it is: there is nothing I professe lesse. These are but my fantasies, by which I endevour not to make things knowen, but my selfe. They may haply one day be knowen unto me, or have bin at other times, according as fortune hath brought me where they were declared or mani-fested. But I remember them no more. And if I be a man of some reading, yet I am a man of no re-membring, I conceive no certainty, except it bee to give notice, how farre the knowledge I have of it, doth now reach. Let no man busie himselfe about the matters, but on the fashion I give them. Let that which I borrow be survaied, and then tell me whether I have made good choice of ornaments, to beautifie and set foorth the invention, which ever comes from mee. For, I make others to relate (not after mine owne fantasie, but as it best falleth out) what I cannot so well expresse, either through unskill of language, or want of judgement. I number not my borrowings, but I weigh them. And if I would have made their number to prevaile, I would have had twice as many. They are all, or almost all of so famous and ancient names, that me thinks they sufficiently name themselves without mee. If in reasons, comparisons and arguments, I transplant any into my soile, or confound them with mine owne, I purposely conceale the Author, thereby to bridle the rashnesse of these hastie censures, that are so head long cast upon all manner of compositions, namely young writings, of men yet living; and in vulgare, that admit all the world to talke of them, and which seemeth to convince the conception and publike designe alike. I will have them to give *Plutarch* a bob upon mine owne lips, and vex themselves, in wronging *Seneca* in mee. My weakenesse must be hidden under such great credits. I will love him that shal trace, or unfeather me; I meane through clearenesse of judgement, and by the onely distinction of the force and beautie of my Discourses. For my selfe, who for want of memorie, am ever to seeke, how to trie and refine them, by the knowledge of their country, knowe perfectly, by measuring mine owne strength, that my soyle is no way capable, of some over-pretious flowers, that therin I find set, and that all the fruits of my encrease could not make it amends. This am I bound to answer-for, if I hinder my selfe, if there be either vanitie, or fault in my Discourses, that I perceive not or am not able to discerne, if they be shewed me. For, many faults doe often escape our eyes; but the infirmitie of judgement consisteth in not being able to perceive them, when another discovereth them unto us. Knowledge and truth may be in us without judgement, and we may have judgement without them: Yea, the acknowledgement of

ignorance, is one of the best and surest testimonies
of judgement that I can finde. I have no other Ser-
geant of band to marshall my rapsodies, than fortune.
And looke how my humours or conceites present
them-selves, so I shuffle them up. Sometimes they
prease out thicke and three-fold, and other times they
come out languishing one by one. I will have my
naturall and ordinarie pace seene as loose, and as
shuffling as it is. As I am, so I goe on plodding. And
besides, these are matters, that a man may not be
ignorant of, and rashly and casually to speake of
them. I would wish to have a more perfect understanding of things, but I will not purchase it so deare,
as it cost. My intention is to passe the remainder of
my life quietly, and not laboriously, in rest, and not
in care. There is nothing I will trouble or vex my selve
about, no not for Science it selfe, what esteeme soever
it be-of. I doe not search and tosse over Books, but
for an honester recreation to please, and pastime to
delight my selfe: or if I studie, I onely endevour to
find out the knowledge that teacheth or handleth the
knowledge of my selfe, and which may instruct me
how to die well, and how to live well.

> *Has meus ad metas sudet oportet equus.*
> PROPERT. iv. *El.* i. 70.

> My horse must sweating runne,
> That this goale may be wonne.

If in reading I fortune to meet with any difficult
points, I fret not my selfe about them, but after I have
given them a charge or two, I leave them as I found
them. Should I earnestly plod upon them I should
loose both time and my selfe; for I have a skipping

wit. What I see not at the first view, I shall lesse see
it, if I opinionate my selfe upon it. I doe nothing
without blithnesse; and an over obstinate continuation and plodding contention, doth dazle, dul and
weary the same: My sight is thereby confounded and
diminished. I must therefore withdraw-it, and at
fittes goe to it againe. Even as to judge well of the
lustre of scarlet we are taught to cast our eyes over it,
in running it over by divers glances, sodaine glimpses,
and reiterated reprisings. If one booke seeme tedious
unto me, I take another, which I follow not with any
earnestnesse, except it be at such houres as I am idle,
or that I am weary with doing nothing. I am not
greatly affected to new books, because ancient Authors
are in my judgement more full and pithy: nor am I
much addicted to Greeke books, forasmuch as my
understanding cannot well rid his worke with a
childish and apprentise intelligence. Amongst moderne
bookes meerly pleasant, I esteeme *Bocace* his *De-
cameron*, *Rabelais*, and the kisses of *John* the second
(if they may be placed under this title) worth the
paines-taking to reade them. As for *Amadis* and such
like trash of writings, they had never the credit so
much as to allure my youth to delight in them. This
I will say more, either boldly or rashly, that this old
and heavie-pased minde of mine, will no more be
pleased with *Aristotle*, or tickled with good *Ovid*: his
facility, and quaint inventions, which heretofore have
so ravished me, they can now a dayes scarcely entertaine me. I speake my minde freely of all things, yea
of such as peradventure exceed my sufficiencie, and
that no way I hold to be of my jurisdiction. What my
conceit is of them, is also to manifest the proportion

of my insight, and not the measure of things. If at
any time I finde my selfe distasted of *Platoes Axiochus*,
as of a forceles worke, due regard had to such an
Author, my judgement doth nothing beleeve it selfe:
It is not so fond-hardy, or selfe-conceited, as it durst
dare to oppose it selfe against the authority of so
many other famous ancient judgements, which he
reputeth his regents and masters, and with whom hee
had rather erre. He chafeth with, and condemneth
himselfe, either to rely on the superficiall sense, being
unable to pierce into the centre, or to view the thing
by some false lustre. He is pleased only to warrant
himselfe from trouble and unrulinesse: As for weaknesse he acknowledgeth and ingeniously avoweth the
same. He thinkes to give a just interpretation to the
apparences which his conception presents unto him,
but they are shallow and imperfect. Most of *Æsopes*
fables have divers senses, and severall interpretations:
Those which *Mythologize* them, chuse some kinde of
colour well-suting with the fable; but for the most
part, it is no other than the first and superficiall glosse:
There are others more quicke, more sinnowie, more
essentiall and more internall, into which they could
never penetrate; and thus thinke I with them. But
to follow my course; I have ever deemed that in
Poesie, *Virgil*, *Lucretius*, *Catullus*, and *Horace*, doe
doubtles by far hold the first ranke: and especially
Virgil in his *Georgiks*, which I esteeme to be the most
accomplished peece of worke of Poesie: In comparison
of which one may easily discerne, that there are some
passages in the *Æneidos*, to which the Author (had
he lived) would no doubt have given some review or
correction: The fifth booke whereof is (in my mind)

the most absolutely perfect. I also love *Lucan*, and willingly read him, not so much for his stile, as for his owne worth, and truth of his opinion and judgement. As for good *Terence*, I allow the quaintnesse and grace of his Latine tongue, and judge him wonderfull conceited and apt, lively to represent the motions and passions of the minde, and the condition of our manners: our actions make me often remember him. I can never reade him so often, but still I discover some new grace and beautie in him. Those that lived about *Virgils* time, complained that some would compare *Lucretius* unto him. I am of opinion, that verily it is an unequall comparison; yet can I hardly assure my selfe in this opinion whensoever I finde my selfe entangled in some notable passage of *Lucretius*. If they were moved at this comparison, what would they say now of the fond, hardy and barbarous stupiditie of those which now adayes compare *Ariosto* unto him? Nay what would *Ariosto* say of it himselfe?

> *O sæclum insipiens et infacetum.*
> <div align="right">Catul. <i>Epig.</i> xliii. 8.</div>
>
> O age that hath no wit,
> And small conceit in it.

I thinke our ancestors had also more reason to cry out against those that blushed not to equall *Plautus* unto *Terence* (who makes more shew to be a Gentleman) than *Lucretius* unto *Virgil*. This one thing doth greatly advantage the estimation and preferring of *Terence*, that the father of the Roman eloquence, of men of his quality doth so often make mention of him; and the censure, which the chiefe Judge of the Roman Poets giveth of his companion. It hath often come

unto my minde, how such as in our dayes give themselves to composing of comedies (as the Italians who
are very happy in them) employ three or foure arguments of *Terence* and *Plautus* to make up one of theirs.
In one onely comedy they will huddle up five or six
of *Bocaces* tales. That which makes them so to charge
themselves with matter, is the distrust they have of
their owne sufficiency, and that they are not able to
undergoe so heavie a burthen with their owne strength.
They are forced to finde a body on which they may
rely and leane themselves: and wanting matter of their
owne wherewith to please us, they will have the story
or tale to busie and ammuse us: where as in my
Author it is cleane contrary: The elegancies, the per-
fections and ornaments of his manner of speech, make
us neglect and lose the longing for his subject. His
quaintnesse and grace doe still retaine us to him. He
is every where pleasantly conceited,

> *Liquidus puroque simillimus amni.*
> > Hor. ii. *Epist*. ii. 120.

> So clearely-neate, so neately-cleare,
> As he a fine-pure River were,

and doth so replenish our minde with his graces, that
we forget those of the fable. The same consideration
drawes me somewhat further. I perceive that good
and ancient Poets have shunned the affectation and
enquest, not only of fantasticall, new fangled, Spagnio-
lized, and Petrarchisticall elevations, but also of more
sweet and sparing inventions, which are the ornament
of all the Poeticall workes of succeeding ages. Yet is
there no competent Judge, that findeth them wanting
in those Ancient ones, and that doth not much more

admire that smoothly equall neatnesse, continued sweetnesse, and flourishing comelinesse of *Catullus* his Epigrams, than all the sharpe quips, and witty girds, wherewith *Martiall* doth whet and embellish the conclusions of his. It is the same reason I spake of erewhile, as *Martiall* of himselfe. *Minus illi ingenio laborandum fuit, in cuius locum materia successerat* (MART. *præf.* viii). *He needed the lesse worke with his wit, in place whereof matter came in supply*; The former without being moved or pricked cause themselves to be heard lowd enough: they have matter to laugh at every where, and need not tickle themselves; where as these must have foraine helpe: according as they have lesse spirit, they must have more body. They leape on horse-backe: because they are not sufficiently strong in their legs to march on foot. Even as in our dances, those base conditioned men that keepe dancing-schooles, because they are unfit to represent the port and decencie of our nobilitie, endevour to get commendation by dangerous lofty trickes, and other strange tumbler-like friskes and motions. And some Ladies make a better shew of their countenances in those dances, wherein are divers changes, cuttings, turnings, and agitations of the body, than in some dances of state and gravity, where they need but simply to tread a naturall measure, represent an unaffected cariage, and their ordinary grace; And as I have also seene some excellent Lourdans, or Clownes attired in their ordinary worky-day clothes, and with a common homely countenance, affoord us all the pleasure that may be had from their art: Prentises and learners that are not of so high a forme, to besmeare their faces, to disguise themselves, and in motions to counterfeit strange visages, and antickes, to enduce us to laughter. This my conception is no where better discerned, than in the comparison between *Virgils Æneidos*, and *Orlando Furioso*. The first is seene to soare aloft with full-spread wings, and with so high and strong a pitch, ever following his point; the other faintly to hover and flutter from tale to tale, and as it were skipping from bough to bough, alwayes distrusting his owne wings, except it be for some short flight, and for feare his strength and breath should faile him, to sit downe at every fields-end.

> *Excursusque breves tentat.*
> VIRG. *Geor*. iv. 194.

> Out-lopes sometimes he doth assay,
> But very short, and as he may.

Loe here then, concerning this kinde of subjects, what Authors please me best: As for my other lesson, which somewhat more mixeth profit with pleasure, whereby I learne to range my opinions, and addresse my conditions; the Bookes that serve me thereunto, are *Plutarke* (since he spake French) and *Seneca*; Both have this excellent commodity for my humour, that the knowledge I seeke in them, is there so scatteringly and loosely handled, that whosoever readeth them is not tied to plod long upon them, whereof I am uncapable. And so are *Plutarkes* little workes, and *Senecas* Epistles, which are the best and most profitable parts of their writings. It is no great matter to draw mee to them, and I leave them where I list. For, they succeed not, and depend not one of another. Both jumpe and suit together, in most true and profitable opinions: And fortune brought them both into the world in one age. Both were Tutors unto two Roman Emperours: Both were strangers, and came from farre Countries; both rich and mighty in the common-wealth, and in credit with their masters. Their instruction is the prime and creame of Philosophy, and presented with a plaine, unaffected, and pertinent fashion. *Plutarke* is more uniforme and constant; *Seneca* more waving and diverse. This doth labour, force, and extend himselfe, to arme and strengthen vertue against weaknesse, feare, and vitious desires; the other seemeth nothing so much to feare their force or attempt, and in a manner scorneth to hasten or change his pace about them, and to put himselfe upon his guard. *Plutarkes* opinions are Platonicall, gentle and accommodable unto civill societie: *Senecaes* Stoicall and Epicurian, further from common use, but in my conceit, more proper, particular, and more solid. It appeareth in *Seneca*, that he somewhat inclineth and yeeldeth to the tyrannie of the Emperors which were in his daies; for, I verily beleeve, it is with a forced judgement, he condemneth the cause of those noblie-minded murtherers of *Cæsar*: *Plutarke* is every where free and open-hearted; *Seneca*, full-fraught with points and sallies, *Plutarke* stuft with matters. The former doth move and enflame you more; the latter, content, please, and pay you better: This doth guide you, the other drive you on. As for *Cicero*, of all his works, those that treat of Philosophie (namely morall) are they which best serve my turne, and square with my intent. But boldly to confesse the trueth, (For, *Since the bars of impudencie were broken downe, all curbing is taken away*) his manner of writing semeth verie tedious unto me, as doth all

such-like stuffe. For, his prefaces, definitions, divi-
sions, and Etymologies, consume the greatest part of
his Works; whatsoever quick, wittie, and pithie conceit is in him, is surcharged, and confounded by those
his long and far-fetcht preambles. If I bestow but one
houre in reading him, which is much for me; and let
me call to minde what substance, or juice I have
drawne from him, for the most part, I find nothing
but wind and ostentation in him: for he is not yet
come to the arguments, which make for his purpose,
and reasons that properly concerne the knot or pith
I seek-after. These Logicall and Aristotelian ordin-
ances are not availfull for me, who onely endevour
to become more wise and sufficient, and not more
wittie or eloquent. I would have one begin with the
last point: I understand sufficiently what death and
voluptuousnesse are: let not a man busie himselfe to
anatomize them. At the first reading of a Booke, I
seeke for good and solid reasons, that may instruct
me how to sustaine their assaults. It is neither gram-
maticall subtilties, nor logicall quiddities, nor the
wittie contexture of choice words, or arguments, and
syllogismes, that will serve my turne. I like those
discourses that give the first charge to the strongest
part of the doubt; his are but flourishes, and languish
every where. They are good for Schooles, at the barre,
or for Orators and Preachers, where we may slumber:
and though we wake a quarter of an houre after, we
may find and trace him soone enough. Such a manner
of speech is fit for those Judges, that a man would
corrupt by hooke or crooke, by right or wrong, or for
children and the common people, unto whom a man
must tell all, and see what the event will be. I would

not have a man go about, and labour by circumlocu-
tions, to induce and win me to attention, and that (as
our Herolds or Criers do) they shall ring out their
words. Now heare me, now listen, or ho-yes. The
Romanes in their Religion were wont to say, *Hoc age*;
which in ours we say, *Sursum corda*. These are so
many lost words for me. I come readie prepared from
my house. I need no allurement nor sawce; my stomacke is good enough to digest raw meat: And
whereas with these preparatives and flourishes, or
preambles, they thinke to sharpen my taste, or stir
my stomacke, they cloy and make it wallowish. Shall
the priviledge of times excuse me from this sacrilegious
boldnesse, to deeme *Platoes* Dialogismes to be as
languishing, by over-filling and stuffing his matter?
And to bewaile the time that a man, who had so many
thousands of things to utter, spends about so many,
so long, so vaine, and idle interloqutions, and preparatives? My ignorance shall better excuse me, in
that I see nothing in the beautie of his language. I
generally enquire after Bookes, that use sciences, and
not after such as institute them. The two first, and
Plinie, with others of their ranke, have no *Hoc age*
in them, they will have to doe with men, that have
forewarned themselves; or if they have, it is a materiall
and substantiall *Hoc age*, and that hath his bodie apart.
I likewise love to read the Epistles and *ad Atticum*,
not onely because they containe a most ample instruction of the Historie, and affaires of his times, but much
more because in them I descrie his private humours.
For, (as I have said elsewhere) I am wonderfull curious,
to discover and know, the minde, the soule, the genuine
disposition, and naturall judgement of my Authors.

A man ought to judge their sufficiencie, and not their customes, nor them by the shew of their writings, which they set forth on this worlds Theatre. I have sorrowed a thousand times, that ever we lost the booke, that *Brutus* writ of Vertue. *Oh it is a goodly thing to learne the Theorike of such as understand the practice well.* But forsomuch as the Sermon is one thing, and the Preacher an other: I live as much to see *Brutus* in *Plutarke*, as in himselfe: I would rather make choice to know certainly, what talke he had in his Tent with some of his familiar friends, the night foregoing the battel, than the speech he made the morrow after to his Armie: and what he did in his chamber or closet, than what in the Senate or market place. As for *Cicero*, I am of the common judgement, that besides learning, there was no exquisite excellencie in him: He was a good Citizen, of an honest-gentle nature, as are commonly fat and burly men; for so was he: But to speake truely of him, full of ambitious vanitie and remisse nicenesse. And I know not well how to excuse him, in that hee deemed his Poesie worthy to be published. It is no great imperfection, to make bad verses, but it is an imperfection in him, that he never perceived how unworthy they were of the glorie of his name. Concerning his eloquence, it is beyond all comparison, and I verily beleeve, that none shall ever equall it. *Cicero* the younger, who resembled his father in nothing, but in name, commanding in *Asia*, chanced one day to have many strangers at his board, and amongst others, one *Cæstius* sitting at the lower end, as the manner is to thrust in at great mens tables: *Cicero* inquired of one of his men what he was, who told him his name, but he dreaming on other matters, and having forgotten what answere his man made him, asked him his name twice or thrice more: the servant, because he would not be troubled to tell him one thing so often, and by some circumstance make him to know him better, It is, said he, the same *Cæstius*, of whom some have told you, that in respect of his owne, maketh no accompt of your fathers eloquence: *Cicero* being suddainly mooved, commaunded the said poore *Cæstius* to be presently taken from the table, and well whipt in his presence; Lo-heere an uncivill and barbarous host. Even amongst those, which (all things considered) have deemed his eloquence matchlesse and incomparable others there have been, who have not spared to note some faults in it: As great *Brutus* said, that it was an eloquence, broken, halting, and disjoynted, *fractam et elumbem: Incoherent and sinnowlesse*. Those Orators that lived about his age, reproved also in him the curious care he had of a certaine long cadence, at the end of his clauses, and noted these words, *Esse videatur*, which he so often useth. As for me, I rather like a cadence that falleth shorter, cut like Iambikes: yet doth he sometimes confound his numbers; but it is seldome: I have especially observed this one place. *Ego vero me minus diu senem esse mallem, quam esse senem, antequam essem* (Cic. *De Senect.*). *But I had rather, not be an old man so long as I might be, than to be old before I should be.* Historians are my right hand; for they are pleasant and easie: and therewithall, the man with whom I desire generally to be acquainted, may more lively and perfectly be discovered in them, than in any other composition: the varietie and truth of his inward con-

ditions, in grosse and by retale: the diversitie of the
meanes of his collection and composing, and of the
accidents that threaten him. Now those that write
of mens lives, forasmuch as they ammuse and busie
themselves more about counsels than events, more
about that which commeth from within, than that
which appeareth outward; they are fittest for me:
And that's the reason why *Plutarke* above all in that
kind, doth best please me. Indeed I am not a little
grieved that we have not a dozen of *Laertii*, or that
he is not more knowne, or better understood: for,
I am not lesse curious to know the fortunes and lives
of these great masters of the world, than to understand
the diversitie of their decrees and conceits. In this
kind of studie of Historie, a man must, without distinction, tosse and turne over all sorts of Authors,
both old and new, both French and others, if he will
learne the things they so diversly treat-of. But me
thinks that *Cæsar* above all doth singularly deserve
to be studied, not onely for the understanding of the
Historie, as of himselfe; so much perfection and excellencie is there in him more than in others, although
Salust be reckoned one of the number. Verily I read
that Author with a little more reverence and respect,
than commonly men reade profane and humane
Workes: sometimes considering him by his actions,
and wonders of his greatnesse, and other times waighing
the puritie and inimitable polishing and elegancie of
his tongue, which (as *Cicero* saith) hath not onely
exceeded all Historians, but haply *Cicero* himselfe:
with such sinceritie in his judgement. Speaking of
his enemies, that except the false colours, wherewith
he goeth about to cloake his bad cause, and the corrup-

tion and filthinesse of his pestilent ambition, I am
perswaded there is nothing in him to be found fault-
with: and that he hath been over-sparing to speak of
himselfe: for, so many notable and great things could
never be executed by him, unlesse he had put more
of his owne unto them, than he setteth downe. I love
those Historians that are either verie simple, or most
excellent. The simple who have nothing of their owne
to adde unto the storie, and have but the care and
diligence to collect whatsoever come unto their
knowledge, and sincerely and faithfully to register all
things, without choice or culling, by the naked truth
leave our judgement more entire, and better satisfied.

Such amongst others (for example sake) plaine and
well-meaning Froisard, who in his enterprize, hath
marched with so free and genuine a puritie, that
having committed some over-sight, he is neither
ashamed to acknowledge, nor afraid to correct the
same, wheresoever he hath either notice or warning of
it: and who representeth unto us the diversitie of the
newes then currant, and the different reports, that
were made unto him. The subject of an historie
should be naked, bare, and formelesse; each man
according to his capacitie or understanding may reap
commoditie out of it. The curious and most excellent
have the sufficiencie to cull and chuse that, which is
worthie to be knowne, and may select of two relations,
that which is most likely: of the condition of Princes,
and of their humors, therby they conclude their
counsels, and attribute convenient words unto them:
they have reason to assume authoritie unto them, to
direct and shapen our beliefe unto theirs. But truly
that belongs not to many. Such as are betweene both

(which is the most common fashion) it is they that
spoile all; they will needs chew our meat for us, and
take upon them a law to judge, and by consequence
to square and encline the storie according to their
fantasie; for, where the judgement bendeth one way,
a man cannot chuse but wrest and turne his narration
that way. They undertake to chuse things worthy to
bee knowne, and now and then conceal either a word
or a secret action from us, which would much better
instruct us: omitting such things as they understand
not, as incredible: and haply such matters, as they
know not how to declare, either in good Latin, or
tolerable French. Let them boldly enstall their eloquence, and discourse: Let them censure at their
pleasure, but let them also give us leave to judge after
them: And let them neither alter nor dispence by their
abridgements and choice, any thing belonging to the
substance of the matter; but let them rather send it
pure and entire with all her dimensions unto us. Most
commonly (as chiefly in our age) this charge of writing
histories is committed unto base, ignorant, and mechanicall kind of people, only for this consideration that
they can speak well; as if we sought to learne the
Grammer of them; and they have some reason, being
only hyred to that end, and publishing nothing but
their tittle-tattle to aime at nothing else so much. Thus
with store of choice and quaint words, and wyre-
drawne phrases they huddle up, and make a hodge-pot
of a laboured contexture of the reports, which they
gather in the market-places, or such other assemblies.
*The only good histories are those that are written by
such as commanded, or were imploied themselves in
weighty affaires, or that were partners in the conduct*

*of them, or that at least have had the fortune to manage
others of like qualitie.* Such in a manner are all the
Græcians and Romans. For, many eye-witnesses
having written of one same subject (as it hapned in
those times, when Greatnesse and Knowledge did
commonly meet) if any fault or oversight have past
them, it must be deemed exceeding light, and upon
some doubtfull accident. *What may a man expect at
a Phisitions hand, that discourseth of warre, or of a
bare Scholler, treating of Princes secret designes?* If
we shall but note the religion, which the Romans had
in that, we need no other example: *Asinius Polio* found
some mistaking or oversight in *Cæsars* Commentaries,
whereinto he was falne, only because he could not
possiblie oversee all things with his owne eyes, that
hapned in his Armie, but was faine to relie on the
reports of particular men, who often related untruths
unto him; or else because he had not been curiously
advertised, and distinctly enformed by his Lieutenants
and Captaines, of such matters as they in his absence
had managed or effected. Whereby may be seen, that
*nothing is so hard, or so uncertaine to be found-out, as
the certaintie of a Truth,* sithence no man can put any
assured confidence concerning the truth of a battel,
neither in the knowledge of him, that was Generall,
or commanded over it, nor in the soldiers that fought,
of any thing, that hath hapned amongst them; except
after the manner of a strict point of law, the severall
witnesses are brought and examined face to face, and
that all matters be nicely and thorowly sifted by the
objects and trials of the successe of every accident.
Verily the knowledge we have of our own affaires is
much more barren and feeble. But this hath sufficiently

been handled by *Bodine*, and agreeing with my conception. Somewhat to aid the weaknesse of my
memorie, and to assist her great defects; for it hath
often been my chance to light upon bookes, which
I supposed to be new, and never to have read, which
I had not understanding diligently read and run-over
many yeares before, and all bescribled with my notes:
I have a while since accustomed my selfe, to note at
the end of my booke (I meane such as I purpose to
read but once) the time I made an end to read it,
and to set downe what censure or judgement I gave
of it; that so, it may at least, at another time represent
unto my mind, the aire and generall Idea, I had con-
ceived of the Author in reading him. I will here set
downe the Copie of some of mine annotations, and
especially what I noted upon my *Guicciardine* about
ten yeares since: (For what language soever my bookes
speake unto me, I speake unto them in mine owne.)
He is a diligent Historiographer, and from whom in
my conceit, a man may as exactly learne the truth of
such affaires as passed in his time, as of any other
writer whatsoever: and the rather because himselfe
hath been an Actor of most part of them, and in verie
honourable place. There is no signe or apparance,
that ever he disguised or coloured any matter, either
through hatred, malice, favour, or vanitie; whereof
the free and impartiall judgements he giveth of great
men, and namely of those by whom he had been
advanced or imployed in his important charges, as of
Pope *Clement* the seaventh, beareth undoubted testimonie. Concerning the parts wherewith he most goeth
about to prevaile which are his digressions and discourses, many of them are verie excellent, and en-

riched with faire ornaments, but he hath too much pleased himselfe in them: for, endevouring to omit nothing that might be spoken, having so full and large a subject, and almost infinite, he proveth somewhat languishing, and giveth a tast of a kind of scholasticall tedious babling. Moreover, I have noted this, that of so severall and divers armes, successes, and effects he judgeth of; of so many and variable motives, alterations, and counsels, that he relateth, he never referreth any one unto vertue, religion, or conscience: as if they were all extinguished and banished the world: and of all actions, how glorious soever in apparance they be of themselves, he doth ever impute the cause of them, to some vicious and blame-worthie occasion, or to some commoditie and profit. It is impossible to imagine, that amongst so infinite a number of actions, whereof he judgeth, some one have not been produced and compassed by way of reason. No corruption could ever possesse men so universally, but that some one must of necessity escape the contagion; which makes me to feare, he hath had some distaste or blame in his passion, and it hath haply fortuned, that he hath judged or esteemed of others according to himselfe. In my *Philip de Comines*, there is this: In him you shall find a pleasing-sweet, and gently-gliding speech, fraught with a purely-sincere simplicitie, his narration pure and unaffected, and wherein the Authours unspotted-good meaning doth evidently appeare, void of all manner of vanitie or ostentation speaking of himselfe, and free from all affection or envie speaking of others: his discourses and perswasions, accompanied more with a well-meaning zeale, and meere veritie, than with any laboured and exquisit sufficiencie, and all-through, with gravitie and authoritie, representing a man well-borne, and brought up in high negotiations. Upon the memories and historie of Monsieur du *Bellay*: It is ever a well-pleasing thing, to see matters writen by those, that have assaid how, and in what manner they ought to be directed and managed: yet can it not be denied, but that in both these Lords, there will manifestly appeare a great declination from a free libertie of writing, which clearely shineth in ancient writers of their kind: as in the Lord of *Jonville*, familiar unto Saint *Lewis*, *Eginard*, Chancellor unto *Charlemaine*; and of more fresh memorie in *Philip de Comines*. This is rather a declamation or pleading for king *Francis* against the Emperour *Charles* the fifth, than an Historie. I will not beleeve, they have altered or changed any thing concerning the generalitie of matters, but rather to wrest and turne the judgement of the events, many times against reason, to our advantage, and to omit whatsoever they supposed, to be doubtfull or ticklish in their masters life: they have made profession of it: witnesse the recoylings of the Lords of *Momorancy* and *Byron*, which therein are forgotten; and which is more, you shall not so much as find the name of the Ladie of Estampes mentioned at all. A man may sometimes colour, and haply hide secret actions, but absolutely to conceal that which all the world knoweth, and especially such things as have drawne-on publike effects, and of such consequence, it is an inexcusable defect, or as I may say unpardonable oversight. To conclude, whosoever desireth to have perfect information and knowledge of King *Francis* the first, and of the things hapned in his time, let him addresse himselfe elsewhere, if he will give any credit unto me. The profit he may reap here, is by the particular deduction of the battels and exploits of warre, wherein these Gentlemen were present; some privie conferences, speeches, or secret actions of some Princes, that then lived, and the practices managed, or negotiations directed by the Lord of *Langeay*, in whom doubtlesse are verie many things, well-worthie to be knowne, and diverse discourses not vulgare.

III. 6.

OF COACHES

It is easie to verifie, that excellent authors, writing of causes do not only make use of those which they imagine true, but eftsoones of such as themselves beleeve not: alwayes provided they have some invention and beautie. They speake sufficiently, truly and profitably, if they speake ingeniously. We cannot assure our selves of the chiefe cause: we hudle up a many together, to see whether by chance it shall be found in that number,

Namque unam dicere causam,
Non satis est, verum plures unde una tamen sit.

LUCR. vi. 703.

Enough it is not one cause to devise,
But more, whereof that one may yet arise.

Will you demand of me, whence this custome ariseth, to blesse an say God helpe to those that sneese? We produce three sortes of winde; that issuing from belowe is too undecent; that from the mouth, implieth some reproach of gourmandise: the third is sneesing:

and because it commeth from the head, and is without
imputation, we thus kindly entertaine it: Smile not
at this subtilty, it is (as some say) *Aristotles*. Me
seemeth to have read in *Plutarch* (who of all the
authors I know, hath best commixt arte with nature,
and coupled judgement with learning) where he
yeeldeth a reason, why those which travell by sea, do
sometimes feele such qualmes and risings of the
stomack, saying, that it proceedeth of a kinde of
feare: having found-out some reason, by which he
prooveth, that feare may cause such an effect. My
selfe who am much subject unto it, know well, that
this cause doth nothing concerne me. And I know it,
not by argument, but by necessary experience, without
alleaging what some have tolde me, that the like doth
often happen unto beasts, namely unto swine, when
they are farthest from apprehending any danger: and
what an acquaintance of mine hath assured me of
himselfe, and who is greatly subject unto it, that twice
or thrice in a tempestuous storme, being surprised
with exceeding feare, all manner of desire or inclina-
tion to vomit had left him. As to that ancient good
fellow; *Pejus vexabar quàm ut periculum mihi suc-
curreret. I was worse vexed then that danger could helpe
me.* I never apprehended feare upon the water; nor
any where else (yet have I often had just cause offred
me, if death it selfe may give it) which either might
trouble or astony me. It proceedeth sometimes as
well from want of judgement, as from lacke of courage.
All the dangers I have had, have beene when mine
eyes were wide-open, and my sight cleare, sound and
perfect: For, *even to feare, courage is required*. It hath
sometimes steaded me, in respect of others, to direct

and keepe my flight in order, that so it might be, if
not without feare, at least without dismay and
astonishment. Indeed it was moved, but not amazed
nor distracted. Undanted mindes march further, and
represent flight, not onely temperate, setled and sound,
but also fierce and bold. Report we that which
Alcibiades relateth of *Socrates* his companion in armes.
I found (saith he) after the route and discomfiture
of our armie, both him and *Lachez* in the last ranke
of those that ranne away, and with all safety and
leasure considered him, for I was mounted upon an
excellent good horse, and he on foote, and so had we
combated all day. I noted first, how in respect of
Lachez: he shewed both discreet judgement and undanted resolution: then I observed the undismaide
bravery of his march, nothing different from his
ordinary pace: his looke orderly and constant, duly
observing and heedily judging what ever passed round
about him: sometimes viewing the one, and sometimes
looking on the other both friends and enemies, with
so composed a manner, that he seemed to encourage
the one and menace the other, signifying, that whosoever should attempt his life, must purchase the same,
or his blood at a high-valued rate? and thus they both
saved themselves; for, men do not willingly graple
with these; but follow such as shew or feare or dismay.
Lo here the testimony of that renowned Captaine,
who teacheth us what wee daily finde by experience,
that there is nothing doth sooner cast us into dangers,
then an inconsiderate greedinesse to avoide them.
*Quo timoris minus est, eo minus fermè periculi est. The
lesse feare there is most commonly, the lesse danger
there is.* Our people is to blame, to say, such a one

feareth death, when it would signifie, that he thinkes
on it, and doth foresee the same. Foresight doth
equally belong as well to that which concerneth us
in good, as touch us in evill. *To consider and judge
danger is in some sort, not to bee danted at it*. I doe not
finde my selfe sufficiently strong to withstand the
blow and violence of this passion of feare, or of any
other impetuosity, were I once therewith vanquished
and deterred, I could never safely recover my selfe.
He that should make my minde forgoe her footing,
could never bring her unto her place againe. She
doth over lively sound, and over deepely search into
her selfe: And therefore never suffers the wound which
pierced the same, to be throughly cured and consoli-
dated. It hath beene happy for me, that no infirmity
could ever yet displace her. I oppose and present
my selfe in the best ward I have, against all charges
and assaults that beset mee. Thus the first that should
beare me away, would make me unrecoverable. I encounter not two: which way soever spoile should enter
my hold, there am I open, and remedilesly drowned.
Epicurus saith, that *a wise man can never passe from
one state to its contrary*. I have some opinion answering
his sentence, that *he who hath once beene a very foole,
shall at no time proove verie wise*. God sends my cold
answerable to my cloths, and passions answering the
meanes I have to indure them. Nature having discovered mee on one side, hath covered mee on the
other. Having disarmed me of strength, she hath
armed me with insensibility, and a regular or soft
apprehension. I cannot long endure (and lesse could
in my youth) to ride either in coach or litter, or to
go in a boat; and both in the Citty and country I hate

all manner of riding, but a horse-back: And can lesse
endure a litter, then a coach, and by the same reason,
more easily a rough agitation upon the water, whence
commonly proceedeth feare, then the soft stirring a
man shall feele in calme weather. By the same easie
gentle motion, which the oares give, convaying the
boat under us, I wot not how, I feele both my head
intoxicated and my stomacke distempered: as I cannot
likewise abide a shaking stoole under me. When as
either the saile, or the gliding course of the water doth
equaly carry us away, or that we are but towed, that
gently gliding and even agitation, doth no whit dis-
temper or hurt me. It is an interrupted and broken
motion, that offends mee; and more when it is languishing. I am not able to display its forme. Phisitions have taught mee to bind and gird my selfe with
a napkin or swath round about the lower part of my
belly, as a remedy for this accident; which as yet I
have not tride, beeing accustomed to wrestle and withstand such defects as are in mee; and tame them by
my selfe. Were my memory sufficiently informed of
them, I would not thinke my time lost, heere to set
down the infinite variety, which histories present unto
us, of the use of coaches in the service of warre: divers
according to the nations, and different according to
the ages: to my seeming of great effect and necessity.
So that it is wondrously strange, how we have lost
all true knowledge of them; I will onely aleadge this,
that even lately in our fathers time, the Hungarians
did very availefully bring them into fashion, and profitably set them a work against the Turks; every one of
them containing a Targattier and a Muskettier, with
a certaine number of harquebuses or calivers, ready

charged; and so ranged, that they might make good
use of them: and all over covered with a pavesado,
after the manner of a Galliotte. They made the front
of their battaile with three thousand such coaches:
and after the Cannon had playd, caused them to
discharge and shoote off a volie of small shott upon
their enemies, before they should know or feele, what
the rest of the forces could doe: which was no small
advancement; or if not this, they mainely drove those
coaches amidde the thickest of their enemies squad-
rons, with purpose to breake, disroute and make waie
through them. Besides the benefit and helpe they
might make of them, in any suspicious or dangerous
place, to flanke their troupes marching from place
to place: or in hast to encompasse, to embarricado,
to cover or fortifie any lodgement or quarter. In my
time, a gentleman of quality, in one of our frontiers,
unwealdy and so burly of body, that hee could finde
no horse able to beare his waight, and having a quarrell
or deadly fude in hand, was wont to travaile up and
downe in a coach made after this fashion, and found
much ease and good in it. But leave we these warlike
coaches, as if their nullity were not sufficiently knowne
by better tokens; The last Kings of our first race were
wont to travell in chariots drawne by foure oxen.
Mark Antonie was the first, that caused himselfe,
accompanied with a minsterell harlot to be drawne
by Lyons fitted to a coach. So did *Heliogabalus* after
him, naming himselfe *Cibele* the mother of the Gods;
and also by Tigers, counterfeiting God *Bacchus*: who
sometimes would also bee drawne in a coach by two
Stagges: and an-other time by foure mastive Dogs:
and by foure naked wenches, causing himselfe to bee

drawne by them in pompe and state, hee being all naked. The emperour *Firmus*, made his coach to bee drawne by Estriges of exceeding greatnesse, so that hee rather seemed to flye, then to roule on wheeles. The strangenesse of these inventions, doth bring this other thing unto my fantasie. That it is a kinde of pusilanimity in Monarkes, and a testimony that they doe not sufficiently know what they are, when they labour to shew their worth, and endevour to appeare unto the world, by excessive and intolerable expences. A thing, which in a strange country might somewhat bee excused; but amongst his native subjects, where hee swayeth all in all, hee draweth from his dignity the extreamest degree of honour, that hee may possible attaine unto. As for a gentleman, in his owne private house to apparrel himselfe richly and curiously, I deeme it a matter vaine and superfluous; his house, his houshold, his traine and his kitchin doe sufficiently answere for him. The counsell which *Isocrates* giveth to his King (in my conceite) seemeth to carry some reason: when hee willeth him to bee richly-stored and stately adorned with mooveables and houshold-stuffe, forsomuch as it is an expence of continuance, and which descendeth even to his posterity or heires: And to avoyde all magnificences, which presently vanish both from custome and memory. I loved when I was a yonger brother to set my selfe foorth and bee gaye in cloathes, though I wanted other necessaries; and it became mee well: There are some on whose backes their rich Robes weepe, or as wee say their rich cloathes are lyned with heavy debts. We have divers strange tales of our auncient Kings frugalitie about their owne persons, and in their gifts: great and farre renouned Kings both in credit, in valour and in fortune. *Demosthenes* mainely combates the law of his Citie, who assigned their publique money to be imployed about the stately setting forth of their playes and feasts: He willeth that their magnificence should bee seene in the quantity of tall ships well manned and appointed, and armies well furnished. And they have reason to accuse *Theophrastus*, who in his booke of riches established a contrarie opinion, and upholdeth such a quality of expences, to be the true fruit of wealth and plenty. They are pleasures (saith *Aristotle*) that onely touch the vulgar and basest communalty, which as soone as a man is satisfied with them, vanish out of minde; and whereof no man of sound judgement or gravity can make any esteeme. The imployment of it, as more profitable, just and durable would seeme more royall, worthy and commendable, about ports, havens, fortifications and walles; in sumptuous buildings, in churches, hospitals, colledges, mending of heighwayes and streetes, and such like monuments: in which things Pope *Gregory* the thirteenth shall leave aye-lasting and commendable memory unto his name: and wherein our Queene *Catherin* should witnes unto succeeding ages her naturall liberality and exceeding bounty, if her meanes were answerable to her affection. Fortune hath much spighted mee to hinder the structure and breake-off the finishing of our new-bridge in our great Citty; and before my death to deprive mee of all hope to see the great necessity of it set forward againe. Moreover, it appeareth unto subjects, spectators of these triumphs, that they have a show made them of their owne riches, and that they are feasted at their proper charges: For, the

people doe easily presume of their kings, as wee doe
of our servants; that they should take care plenteously
to provide us of whatsoever wee stand in neede of,
but that on their behalfe they should no way lay hands
on it. And therefore the Emperor *Galba*, sitting at
supper, having taken pleasure to heare a musician
play and sing before him, sent for his casket, out of
which he tooke a handful of Crownes and put them into
his hand, with these wordes, *Take this, not as a gift of
the publique money, but of mine owne private store.* So
is it, that it often commeth to passe, that the common
people have reason to grudge, and that their eyes are
fedde, with that which should feede their belly.
Liberality it selfe, in a soveraigne hand is not in her
owne luster: private men have more right, and may
challenge more interest in her. For, taking the matter
exactly as it is, *a King hath nothing that is properly his
owne; hee oweth even himselfe to others. Authority is
not given in favour of the authorising, but rather in
favour of the authorised. A superiour is never created
for his owne profit, but rather for the benefit of the in-
feriour: And a Phisition is instituted for the sicke, not
for himselfe. All Magistracie, even as each arte, rejecteth her end out of her selfe. Nulla ars in se versatur.
No arte is all in it selfe.* Wherefore the governours
and overseers of Princes childhood or minority, who
so earnestly endeavor to imprint this vertue of bounty
and liberality in them; and teach them not to refuse
any thing, and esteeme nothing so well imployed, as
what they shall give (an instruction which in my dayes
I have seene in great credit) either they preferre and
respect more their owne profit than their masters;
or else they understand not aright to whom they

speake. It is too easie a matter to imprint liberality
in him, that hath wherewith plenteously to satisfie
what he desireth at other mens charges. And his
estimation being directed not according to the measure
of the present, but according to the quality of his
meanes, that exerciseth the same, it commeth to
prove vaine in so puissant hands. They are found to
bee prodigall, before they be liberall. Therefore it is
but of small commendation, in respect of other royall
vertues. And the onely (as said the tyrant *Dionysius*)
that agreed and squared well with tyrannie it selfe.
I would rather teach him the verse of the ancient
labourer,

> τῇ χειρὶ δεῖ σπείρειν ἀλλὰ μὴ ὅλῳ τῷ θυλακῷ.
>
> Not whole sackes, but by the hand
> A man should sow his seed i' the land.
>
> PLUT. *De Athen.*
> ERAS. *Chil.* iii. cent. i. ad. 32.

That whosoever will reape any commodity by it,
must sow with his hand, and not powre out of the
sacke: that *corne must be discreetly scattered, and not
lavishly dispersed*: And that being to give, or to say
better, to pay and restore to such a multitude of
people, according as they have deserved, he ought to
be a loyall, faithfull, and advised distributor thereof.
If the liberality of a Prince be without heedy discretion
and measure, I would rather have him covetous and
sparing. *Princely vertue seemeth to consist most in
justice.* And of all parts of justice, that doth best and
most belong to Kings, which accompanieth liberality.
For they have it particularly reserved to their charge;
whereas all other justice, they happily exercise the

same by the intermission of others. *Immoderate bounty is a weake meane to acquire them good will*: for it rejecteth more people than it obtaineth: *Quo in plures usus sis, minus in multos uti possis. Quid autem est stultius, quàm, quod libenter facias, curare ut id diutius facere non possis?* (CIC. *Off.* i). *The more you have used it to many, the lesse may you use it to many more: And what is more fond than what you willingly would not doe, to provide you can no longer doe it?* And if it be emploied without respect of merit, it shameth him that receiveth the same, and is received without grace. Some Tyrants have been sacrificed to the peoples hatred, by the very hands of those, whom they had rashly preferred and wrongfully advanced: such kinde of men, meaning to assure the possession of goods unlawfully and indirectly gotten, if they shew to hold in contempt and hatred, him from whom they held them, and in that combine themselves unto the vulgar judgement and common opinion. *The subjects of a Prince, rashly excessive in his gifts, become impudently excessive in begging*: they adhere, not unto reason, but unto example. Verily we have often just cause to blush, for our impudency. We are over-paid according to justice, when the recompence equaleth our service: for, doe we not owe a kinde of naturall duty to our Princes? If he beare our charge, he doth overmuch; it sufficeth if hee assist it: the over-plus is called a benefit, which cannot be exacted; for the very name of liberality implyeth liberty. After our fashion we have never done; what is received is no more reckoned of: onely future liberality is loved: Wherefore *the more a Prince doth exhaust himselfe in giving, the more friends he impoverisheth*. How should he satisfie intemperate desires, which increase according as they are replenished? *Who so hath his minde on taking, hath it no more on what he hath taken. Covetousnesse hath nothing so proper, as to bee ungratefull.* The example of *Cyrus* shal not ill fit this place, for the behoofe of our kings of these daies, as a touch-stone, to know whether their gifts be wel or ill employed; and make them perceive how much more happily that Emperour did wound and oppresse them, than they doe. Whereby they are afterward forced to exact and borrow of their unknowne subjects, and rather of such as they have wronged and aggrieved, then of those they have enriched and done good unto: and receive no aids, where any thing is gratitude, except the name. *Crœsus* upbraided him with his lavish bounty, and calculated what his treasure would amount unto, if he were more sparing and close-handed. A desire surprised him to justifie his liberality, and dispatching letters over all parts of his dominions, to such great men of his estate, whom hee had particularly advanced, intreated every one to assist him with as much money as they could, for an urgent necessitie of his; and presently to send it him by declaration: when all these count-bookes or notes were brought him, each of his friends supposing that it sufficed not, to offer him no more than they had received of his bounteous liberality, but adding much of their owne unto it, it was found, that the said summe amounted unto much more than the niggardly sparing of *Crœsus.* Whereupon *Cyrus* said, *I am no lesse greedy of riches, than other Princes, but I am rather a better husband of them. You see with what small venture I have purchased the unvaluable treasure of so many friends, and how much more faithfull treasurers they are to mee, than mercenary men would be, without obligation and without affection: and my ex-chequer or treasury better placed than in paltery coafers; by which I draw upon me the hate, the envy and the contempt of other Princes.* The ancient Emperours were wont to draw som excuse, for the superfluity of their sports and publike shewes, for so much as their authority did in some sort depend (at least in appar-ance) from the will of the Romane people; which from all ages are accustomed to be flattered by such kinde of spectacles and excesse.

But they were particular ones who had bred this custome, to gratifie their con-citizens and fellowes: especially by their purse, by such profusion and magni-ficence. It was cleane altered, when the masters and chiefe rulers came once to imitate the same. *Pecuni-arum translatio à justis dominis ad alienos non debet liberalis videri* (CIC. *Off.* i). *The passing of money from right owners to strangers should not seeme liberality. Philip,* because his sonne indeavoured by gifts to purchase the good will of the Macedonians, by a letter seemed to be displeased, and chid him in this manner: What? *Wouldest thou have thy subjects to account thee for their purse-bearer, and not repute thee for their King? Wilt thou frequent and practise them? Then doe it with the benefits of thy vertue, not with those of thy cofers*: Yet was it a goodly thing to cause a great quantity of great trees, all branchie and greene, to bee far brought and planted in plots yeelding nothing but dry gravell, representing a wilde shady forrest, divided in due seemly proportion: And the first day, to put into the same a thousand Estriges, a thousand

Stagges, a thousand wilde Boares, and a thousand
Buckes, yeelding them over to bee hunted and killed
by the common people: the next morrow in the presence of all the assembly to cause a hundred great
Lions, a hundred Leopards, and three hundred huge
Beares to be baited and tugged in pieces: and for the
third day, in bloody manner and good earnest to make
three hundred couple of Gladiators or Fencers, to
combate and murder one another; as did the Emperour
Probus. It was also a goodly shew, to see those huge
Amphitheaters all enchased with rich marble, on the
outside curiously wrought with carved statues, and
all the inner side glittering with precious and rare
embellishments.

> *Baltheus en gemmis, en illita porticus auro.*

> A belt beset with gemmes behold,
> Behold a walke bedawb'd with gold.

All the sides round about that great void, replenished
and invironed from the ground unto the very top, with
three or fourescore rankes of steps and seates, likewise
all of marble covered with faire cushions,

> *—exeat, inquit,*
> *Si pudor est, et de pulvino surgat equestri,*
> *Cujus res legi non sufficit.*—Juven. *Sat.* iii. 153.

> If shame there be, let him be gone, he cries,
> And from his knightly cushion let him rise,
> Whose substance to the law doth not suffice.

Where might conveniently bee placed an hundred
thousand men, and all sit at ease. And the plaine-
groundworke of it, where sports were to be acted,
first by Art to cause the same to open and chap in

sunder with gaps and cranishes, representing hollow
cavernes which vomited out the beasts appointed for
the spectacle: that ended, immediately to overflow it
all with a maine deepe sea, fraught with store of sea-
monsters and other strange fishes, all over-laid with
goodly tall ships, ready rigd and appointed to represent
a Sea-fight; and thirdly, suddenly to make it smooth
and drie againe, for the combate of Gladiators: and
fourthly, being forthwith cleansed, to strewe it over
with Vermilion and Storax, insteede of gravell, for
the erecting of a solemne banket, for all that infinite
number of people: the last act of one onely day.

> —*quoties nos descendentis arenæ*
> *Vidimus in partes, ruptaque voragine terræ*
> *Emersisse feras, et iisdem sæpe latebris*
> *Aurea cum croceo creverunt arbuta libro.*
> *Nec solum nobis silvestria cernere monstra*
> *Contigit, equoreos ego cum certantibus ursis*
> *Spectavi vitulos, et equorum nomine dignum,*
> *Sed deforme pecus.*

How oft have we beheld wild beasts appeare
From broken gulfes of earth, upon some parte
Of sande that did not sinke? how often there
And thence did golden boughs ore saffron'd starte?
Nor onely saw we monsters of the wood,
But I have seene Sea-calves whom Beares withstood,
And such a kinde of beast as might be named
A horse, but in most foule proportion framed.

They have sometimes caused an high steepy moun-
taine to arise in the midst of the sayd Amphitheaters,
all overspred with fruitfull and flourishing trees of
all sortes, on the top whereof gushed out streames of
water, as from out the source of a purling spring.

Other times they have produced a great tall Ship
floating up and downe, which of it selfe opened and
split a sunder, and after it had disgorged from out it's
bulke, foure or five hundred wild beasts to bee baited,
it closed and vanished away of it selfe, without any
visible helpe. Sometimes from out the bottome of it,
they caused streakes and purlings of sweete water to
spoute up, bubling to the highest top of the frame,
and gently watring, sprinkling and refreshing that
infinite multitude. To keepe and cover themselves
from the violence of the wether, they caused that
huge compasse to be all over-spred, sometimes with
purple sailes, all curiously wrought with the needle,
sometimes of silke, and of some other colour, in the
twinkling of an eye, as they pleased, they displaid
and spred, or drewe and pulled them in againe.

> *Quamvis non modico caleant spectacula sole*
> *Vela reducuntur cum venit Hermogenes.*
>
> MART. xii. *Epig.* 29, 15.

> Though fervent Sunne make't hotte to see a play,
> When linnen thieves come, sailes are kept away.

The nets likewise, which they used to put before
the people, to save them from harme and violence of
the baited beasts, were woven with golde.

> —*auro quoque torta refulgent*
> *Retia.*
>
> Nets with gold enterlaced,
> Their shewes with glittring graced.

If any thing bee excusable in such lavish excesse,
it is, where the invention and strangenesse breedeth
admiration, and not the costlie charge. Even in those

vanities, wee may plainely perceive how fertile and happy those former ages were of other manner of wittes, then ours are. It hapneth of this kinde of fertilitie as of all other productions of nature. Wee may not say what nature employed then the utmost of hir power. We goe not, but rather creepe and stagger here and there: we goe our pace. I imagine our knowledge to bee weake in all senses: *wee neither discerne far-forward, nor see much backward.* It embraceth little, and liveth not long: It is short both in extension of time, and in amplenesse of matter or invention.

> *Vixere fortes ante Agamemnona*
> *Multi, sed omnes illachrymabiles*
> *Urgentur, ignotique longa*
> *Nocte.*—Hor. *Car.* iv. *Od.* ix. 25.

> Before great *Agamemnon* and the rest,
> Many liv'd valiant, yet are all supprest,
> Unmoan'd, unknowne, in darke oblivions nest.

> *Et supera bellum Trojanum et funera Trojæ,*
> *Multi alias alii quoque res cecinere poetæ.*
> > Lucr. v. 327.

> Beside the Trojan warre, *Troyes* funerall night,
> Of other things did other Poets write.

And *Solons* narration concerning what he had learned of the Ægyptian Priests, of their states long-life, and and manner how to learne and preserve strange or forraine histories, in mine opinion is not a testimony to bee refused in this consideration. *Si interminatam in omnes partes magnitudinem regionum videremus, et temporum, in quam se injiciens animus et intendens, ita latè longeque peregrinatur, ut nullam oram ultimi videat, in qua possit insistere: In hæc immensitate infinita, vis innumerabilium appareret formarum* (CIC. *Nat. Deo.* i). *If we behold an unlimited greatnesse on all sides both of regions and times, whereupon the mind casting it selfe and intentive doth travell farre and neare, so as it sees no bounds of what is last, whereon it may insist; in this infinite immensity there would appeare a multitude of innumerable formes.* If whatsoever hath come unto us by report of what is past were true, and knowne of any body, it would be lesse then nothing, in respect of that which is unknowne. And even of this image of the world, which whilest we live therein, glideth and passeth away, how wretched, weake and how short is the knowledge of the most curious? Not onely of the particular events, which fortune often maketh exemplar and of consequence: but of the state of mighty common-wealths, large Monarkies and re-nowned nations, there escapeth our knowledge a hundred times more, then commeth unto our notice. We keepe a coile, and wonder at the miraculous invention of our artilerie, and amazed at the rare devise of Printing: when as unknowne to us, other men, and an other end of the world named *China*, knew and had perfect use of both, a thousand yeares before. *If we sawe as much of this vaste world, as we see but a least part of it, it is very likely we should perceive a perpetuall multiplicity, and ever-rouling vicissitude of formes. Therein is nothing singular, and nothing rare, if regard bee had unto nature, or to say better, if relation bee had unto our knowledge:* which is a weake foundation of our rules, and which doth commonly present us a right-false Image of things. How vainely do we now-adayes conclude the declination and decrepitude of the world, by the fond arguments wee drawe from our owne weakenesse, drooping and declination:

Jamque adeo affecta est ætas, affectaque tellus:
LUCR. ii. 1150.

And now both age and land
So sicke affected stand.

And as vainly did another conclude it's birth and youth, by the vigour he perceiveth in the wits of his time, abounding in novelties and invention of divers Arts:

Verùm ut opinor, habet novitatem, summa, recensque
Natura est mundi, neque pridem exordia cepit:
Quare etiam quædam nunc artes expoliuntur,
Nunc etiam augescunt, nunc addita navigiis sunt
Multa.—Ibid. v. 331.

But all this world is new, as I suppose,
Worlds nature fresh, nor lately it arose:
Whereby some arts refined are in fashion,
And many things now to our navigation
Are added, daily growne to augmentation.

Our world hath of late discovered another (and who can warrant us whether it be the last of his brethren, since both the *Damons*, the *Sibylles*, and all we have hitherto been ignorant of this?) no lesse-large, fully-peopled, all-things-yeelding, and mighty in strength, than ours: neverthelesse so new and infantine, that he is yet to learne his A.B.C. It is not yet full fifty yeeres that he knew neither letters, nor waight, nor measures, nor apparell, nor corne, nor vines. But was all naked, simply-pure, in Natures lappe, and lived but with such meanes and food as his mother-nurce affoorded him. If wee conclude aright of our

end, and the foresaid Poet of the infancie of his age,
this late-world shall but come to light, when ours shall
fall into darknesse. The whole Universe shall fall into
a palsey or convulsion of sinnowes: one member shall
be maimed or shrunken, another nimble and in good
plight. I feare, that by our contagion, we shall directly
have furthered his declination, and hastened his ruine;
and that we shall too dearely have sold him our
opinions, our new-fangles and our Arts. It was an
unpolluted, harmelesse infant world; yet have we not
whipped and submitted the same unto our discipline,
or schooled him by the advantage of our valour or
naturall forces, nor have wee instructed him by our
justice and integrity; nor subdued by our magna-
nimity. Most of their answers, and a number of the
negotiations we have had with them, witnesse that
they were nothing short of us, nor beholding to us
for any excellency of naturall wit or perspicuitie, concerning pertinency. The wonderfull, or as I may call
it, amazement-breeding magnificence of the never-
like seene Cities of *Cusco* and *Mexico*, and amongst
infinite such like things, the admirable Garden of that
King, where all the Trees, the fruits, the Hearbes
and Plants, according to the order and greatnesse they
have in a Garden, were most artificially framed in
gold: as also in his Cabinet, all the living creatures
that his Countrey or his Seas produced, were cast in
gold; and the exquisite beauty of their workes, in
precious Stones, in Feathers, in Cotton and in
Painting: shew that they yeelded as little unto us in
cunning and industrie. But concerning unfained
devotion, awefull observance of lawes, unspotted
integrity, bounteous liberality, due loyalty and free

liberty, it hath greatly availed us, that we had not so much as they: By which advantage, they have lost, cast-away, sold, undone and betraied themselves.

Touching hardinesse and undaunted courage, and as for matchlesse constancie, unmooved assurednesse, undismaied resolution against paine, smarting, famine and death it selfe; I will not feare to oppose the examples which I may easily finde amongst them, to the most famous ancient examples, we may with all our industrie discover in all the Annales and memories of our knowen old World. For, as for those which have subdued them, let them lay aside the wiles, the policies and stratagems, which they have emploied to cozen, to cunny-catch, and to circumvent them; and the just astonishment which those nations might justly conceive, by seeing so unexpected an arrivall of bearded men; divers in language, in habite, in religion, in behaviour, in forme, in countenance; and from a part of the world so distant, and where they never heard any habitation was: mounted upon great and unknowen monsters; against those, who had never so much as seene any horse, and lesse any beast whatsoever apt to beare, or taught to carry either man or burden; covered with a shining and hard skinne, and armed with slicing-keene weapons and glittering armour: against them, who for the wonder of the glistring of a looking-glasse or of a plaine knife, would have changed or given inestimable riches in Gold, Precious Stones and Pearles; and who had neither the skill nor the matter wherewith at any leasure, they could have pierced our steele; to which you may adde the flashing-fire and thundring roare of shotte and Harguebuses; able to quell and daunt even *Cæsar* himselfe, had he beene so sodainely surprised and as little experienced as they were: and thus to come unto, and assault silly-naked people, saving where the invention of weaving of Cotton cloath was knowne and used: for the most altogether unarmed, except some bowes, stones, staves and woodden bucklers: unsuspecting poore people, surprised under colour of amity and well-meaning faith over-taken by the curiosity to see strange and unknowne things: I say take this disparity from the conquerors, and you deprive them of all the occasions and cause of so many unexpected victories. When I consider that sterne-untamed obstinacy, and undanted vehemence, where-with so many thousands of men, of women and children, do so infinite times present themselves unto inevitable dangers, for the defence of their Gods and liberty: This generous obstinacy to endure all extremities, all difficulties and death, more easily and willingly, then basely to yeelde unto their domination, of whom they have so abhominably beene abused: some of them choosing rather to starve with hunger and fasting, being taken, then to accept food at their enemies hands, so basely victorious: I perceave, that whosoever had undertaken them man to man, without ods of armes, of experience or of number, should have had as dangerous a warre, or perhaps more, as any we see amongst us.

Why did not so glorious a conquest happen under *Alexander*, or during the time of the ancient Greekes and Romanes? or why befell not so great a change and alteration of Empires and people, under such hands as would gently have polished, reformed and in-civilized, what in them they deemed to be barbarous

and rude: or would have nourished and fostered those
good seedes, which nature had there brought foorth:
adding not onely to the manuring of their grounds and
ornaments of their cities, such artes as we had; and
that no further then had beene necessary for them,
but therewithall joyning unto the originall vertues of
the country, those of the ancient Grecians and Romanes?
What reparation and what reformation would all that
farre spredding world have found, if the examples,
demeanors and pollicies, wherewith we first presented
them, had called and allured those uncorrupted nations,
to the admiration and imitation of vertue, and had
established betweene them and us a brotherly society
and mutuall correspondency? How easie a matter
had it beene, profitably to reforme, and christianly
to instruct, minds yet so pure and new, so willing to
bee taught, being for the most part endowed with so
docile, so apt and so yeelding naturall beginnings?
whereas contrarywise, we have made use of their
ignorance and inexperience, to drawe them more
easily unto treason, fraude, luxurie, avarice and all
manner of inhumanity and cruelty, by the example of
our life and patterne of our customes. Who ever
raised the service of marchandize and benefit of
traffick to so high a rate? So many goodly citties
ransacked and razed; so many nations destroyed and
made desolate; so infinite millions of harmelesse
people of all sexes, states and ages, massacred, ravaged
and put to the sword; and the richest, the fairest and
the best part of the world topsiturvied, ruined and
defaced for the traffick of Pearles and Pepper: Oh
mechanicall victories, oh base conquest. Never did
greedy revenge, publik wrongs or generall enmities,

so moodily enrage, and so passionately incense men
against men, unto so horrible hostilities, bloody dissi-
pation, and miserable calamities.

Certaine Spaniardes coasting alongst the Sea in
search of mines, fortuned to land in a very fertile,
pleasant and well peopled country: unto the inhabitants whereof they declared their intent, and shewed
their accustomed perswasions; saying: That they were
quiet and well-meaning men, comming from farre-
countries, being sent from the King of *Castile*, the
greatest King of the habitable earth, unto whom the
Pope, representing God on earth, had given the prin-
cipality of all the *Indies*. That if they would become
tributaries to him, they should bee most kindly used
and courteously entreated: They required of them
victualles for their nourishment; and some gold for
the behoofe of certaine Physicall experiments. Moreover, they declared unto them, the beleeving in one
onely God, and the trueth of our religion, which they
perswaded them to embrace, adding thereto some
minatorie threates. Whose answer was this: That
happily they might be quiet and well meaning, but their
countenance shewed them to be otherwise: As concerning
their King, since he seemed to beg, he shewed to be
poore and needy: And for the Pope, who had made that
distribution, he expressed himselfe a man loving dissen-
tion, in going about to give unto a third man, a thing
which was not his owne: so to make it questionable and
litigious amongst the ancient possessors of it. As for
victualles, they should have part of their store: And for
gold, they had but little, and that it was a thing they
made very small accoumpt of, as meerely unprofitable for
the service of their life, whereas all their care was but

how to passe it happily and pleasantly: and therefore,
what quantity soever they should finde, that onely ex-
cepted which was employed about the service of their
Gods, they might bouldly take it. As touching one onely
God, the discourse of him had very well pleased them:
but they would by no meanes change their religion,
under which they had for so long time lived so happily:
and that they were not accustomed to take any counsell,
but of their friends and acquaintance. As concerning
their menaces, it was a signe of want of judgement, to
threaten those, whose nature, condition, power and
meanes was to them unknowne. And therefore they
should with all speed hasten to avoid their dominions
(forsomuch as they were not wont to admit or take in
good part the kindnesses and remonstrances of armed
people, namely of strangers) otherwise they would deale
with them as they had done with such others, shewing
them the heads of certaine men sticking upon stakes
about their Citie, which had lately beene executed. Loe
here an example of the stammering of this infancy.

But so it is, neither in this, nor in infinite other
places, where the Spaniards found not the marchan-
dise they sought for, neither made stay or attempted
any violence, whatsoever other commodity the place
yeelded: witnesse my Canibales. Of two the most
mighty and glorious Monarkes of that world, and peradventure of all our Westerne parts, Kings over so
many Kings: the last they deposed and overcame: He
of *Peru*, having by them been taken in a battell, and
set at so excessive a ransome, that it exceedeth all
beliefe, and that truely paide: and by his conversation
having given them apparant signes of a free, liberall,
undanted and constant courage, and declared to be

of a pure, noble, and well composed understanding; a humour possessed the conquerors, after they had most insolently exacted from him a Million, three hundred five and twenty thousand, and five hundred waights of golde; besides the silver and other precious things, which amounted to no lesse a summe (so that their horses were all shood of massive gold) to discover (what disloyalty or treachery soever it might cost them) what the remainder of this Kings treasure might be, and without controlment enjoy what ever he might have hidden or concealed from them. Which to compasse, they forged a false accusation and proofe against him; That hee practised to raise his provinces, and intended to induce his subjects to some insurrection, so to procure his liberty. Whereupon, by the very judgement of those who had complotted this forgery and treason against him, hee was condemned to be publikely hanged and strangled: having first made him to redeeme the torment of being burned alive, by the baptisme which at the instant of his execution, in charity they bestowed upon him. A horrible and the like never heard of accident: which neverthelesse he undismaiedly endured with an unmoved manner, and truly-royall gravity, without ever contradicting himselfe either in countenance or speech. And then, somewhat to mitigate and circumvent those silly unsuspecting people, amazed and astonished at so strange a spectacle, they counterfeited a great mourning and lamentation for his death, and appointed his funeralls to bee solemnly and sumptuously celebrated.

The other King of *Mexico*, having a long time manfully defended his besieged City, and in the tedious

siege, shewed what ever pinching-sufferance, and
resolute-perseverance can effect, if ever any couragious
Prince or warre-like people shewed the same; and his
disastrous successe having delivered him alive into
his enemies hands, upon conditions to bee used as
beseemed a King: who during the time of his im-
prisonment, did never make the least shew of any
thing unworthy that glorious title. After which victory, the Spaniards not finding that quantitie of gold
they had promised themselves, when they had ransacked and ranged all corners, they by meanes of the
cruellest tortures and horriblest torments they could
possibly devise, beganne to wrest and draw some more
from such prisoners as they had in keeping. But unable
to profit any thing that way, finding stronger hearts
than their torments, they in the end fell to such moody
outrages, that contrary to all law of nations, and against
their solemne vowes and promises, they condemned
the King himselfe and one of the chiefest Princes of
his Court, to the Racke, one in presence of another:
The Prince environed round with hot burning coales,
being overcome with the exceeding torment, at last
in most pitious sort turning his dreary eyes toward
his Master, as if hee asked mercy of him for that hee
could endure no longer; The king fixing rigorously
and fiercely his lookes upon him, seeming to upbraid
him with his remisnesse and pusilanimity, with a
sterne and setled voyce uttered these few words unto
him: *What? supposest thou I am in a cold bath? am I
at more ease than thou art?* Whereat the silly wretch
immediately fainted under the torture, and yeelded
up the ghost. The king half rosted was carried away:
Not so much for pitty (for what ruth could ever enter

so barbarous mindes, who upon the surmised information of some odde piece or vessell of golde, they intended to get, would broyle a man before their eyes, and not a man onely, but a king, so great in fortune and so renowned in desert?) but for as much as his unmatched constancy did more and more make their inhumane cruelty ashamed: They afterward hanged him, because he had couragiously attempted by armes to deliver himselfe out of so long captivity and miserable subjection; where he ended his wretched life, worthy an high minded and never danted Prince. At another time, in one same fire, they caused to be burned all alive foure hundred common men, and threescore principall Lords of a Province, whom by the fortune of warre they had taken prisoners. These narrations we have out of their owne bookes: for they doe not onely avouch, but vauntingly publish them. *May it bee, they doe it for a testimony of their justice or zeale toward their religion?* verily they are wayes overdifferent and enemies to so sacred an ende. Had they proposed unto themselves to enlarge and propagate our religion, they would have considered, that it is not amplified by possession of lands, but of men: and would have beene satisfied with such slaughters, as the necessity of warre bringeth, without indifferently adding thereunto so bloody a butchery, as upon savage beasts; and so universall as fire or sword could ever attaine unto; having purposely preserved no more than so many miserable bond-slaves, as they deemed might suffice for the digging, working and service of their mines: So that divers of their chieftains have beene executed to death, even in the places they had conquered, by the appointment of the Kings of *Castile*,

justly offended at the seld-seene horror of their barbarous demeanours, and well nigh all disesteemed,
contemned and hated. God hath meritoriously per-
mitted, that many of their great pillages, and ill gotten
goods, have either beene swallowed up by the revenging
Seas in transporting them, or consumed by the intestine
warres and civill broiles, wherewith themselves have
devoured one another; and the greatest part of them
have been over-whelmed and buried in the bowels of
the earth, in the very places they found them, without
any fruit of their victory. Touching the objection which
some make, that the receipt, namely in the hands of
so thrifty, wary and wise a Prince, doth so little answer
the fore-conceived hope, which was given unto his
predecesors, and the said former aboundance of
riches, they met withall at the first discovery of this
new-found world, (for although they bring home
great quantity of gold and silver, we perceive the
same to be nothing, in respect of what might be ex-
pected thence) it may be answered, that the use of
money was there altogether unknowne; and consequently, that all their gold was gathered together,
serving to no other purpose, than for shew, state and
ornament, as a moovable reserved from father to
sonne by many puissant Kings, who exhausted all
their mines, to collect so huge a heape of vessels or
statues for the ornament of their Temples, and em-
bellishing of their Pallaces: whereas all our gold is
employed in commerce and trafficke betweene man
and man. Wee mince and alter it into a thousand
formes: wee spend, wee scatter and disperse the same
to severall uses. Suppose our Kings should thus gather
and heape up all the gold they might for many ages

hoard up together, and keepe it close and untouched. Those of the kingdome of *Mexico* were somewhat more encivilized, and better artists, than other nations of that world. And as wee doe, so judged they, that this Universe was neare his end: and tooke the desolation wee brought amongst them as an infallible signe of it. They beleeved the state of the world, to bee divided into five ages, as in the life of five succeeding Sunnes, whereof foure had already ended their course or time; and the same which now shined upon them, was the fifth and last. The first perished together with all other creatures, by an universall inundation of waters. The second by the fall of the heavens upon us which stifled and overwhelmed every living thing: in which age they affirme the Giants to have beene, and shewed the Spaniards certaine bones of them, according to whose proportion the stature of men came to bee of the height of twenty handfuls. The third was consumed by a violent fire, which burned and destroyed all. The fourth by a whirling emotion of the ayre and windes, which with the violent fury of it selfe, remooved and overthrew divers high mountaines: saying, that men dyed not of it, but were transformed into Munkies. (*Oh what impressions doth not the weakenesse of mans beliefe admit?*) After the consummation of this fourth Sunne, the world continued five and twenty yeares in perpetuall darkenesse: in the fifteenth of which one man and one woman were created, who renewed the race of man-kinde. Ten yeares after, upon a certaine day, the Sunne appeared as newly created: from which day beginneth ever since the calculation of their yeares. On the third day of whose creation, died their ancient Gods, their

new ones have day by day beene borne since. In what
manner this last Sunne shall perish, my aucthor could
not learne of them. But their number of this fourth
change, doth jumpe and meete with that great con-
junction of the Starres, which eight hundred and odde
yeares since, according to the Astrologians suppposi-
tion, produced divers great alterations and strange
novelties in the world. Concerning the proud pompe
and glorious magnificence, by occasion of which I am
fallen into this discourse, nor *Grece*, or *Rome*, nor
Ægipt, can (bee it in profit, or difficultie or nobility)
equall or compare sundrie and divers of their workes.
The cawcy or high-way which is yet to bee seene in
Peru, erected by the Kings of that countrie, stretching
from the city of *Quito*, unto that of *Cusco* (containing
three hundred leagues in length) straight, even, and
fine, and twentie paces in breadth curiously paved,
raysed on both sides with goodly, high masonrie-
walles, all along which, on the inner side there are
two continuall running streames, pleasantly beset
with beautious trees, which they call *Moly*. In framing
of which, where they mette any mountaines or rockes,
they have cut, rased and levelled them, and filled all
hollow places with lime and stone. At the ende of
every dayes journey, as stations, there are built stately
great pallaces, plentiously stored with all manner of
good victuals, apparrell and armes, as well for daylie
way-fairing men, as for such armies that might happen
to passe that way. In the estimation of which worke
I have especially considered the difficulty, which in
that place is particularly to bee remembred. For they
built with no stones that were lesse than ten foote
square: They had no other meanes to cary or trans-

port them, then by meere strength of armes to draw
and dragge the carriage they needed: they had not so
much as the arte to make scaffolds; nor knew other
devise, then to raise so much earth or rubbish, against
their building, according as the worke riseth, and
afterward to take it away againe. But returne we to
our coaches. In steade of them, and of all other
carrying beastes they caused themselves to be carryed
by men, and upon their shoulders. This last King
of *Peru*, the same day hee was taken, was thus carried
upon rafters or beames of massive Golde, sitting in
a faire chaire of state, likewise all of golde, in the
middle of his battaile. Looke how many of his porters
as were slaine, to make him fall (for all their endevour
was to take him alive) so many others, and as it were
avye, tooke and underwent presently the place of the
dead: so that they could never be brought down or
made to falle, what slaughter so ever was made of
those kinde of people, untill such time as a horseman
furiously ranne to take him by some part of his body,
and so pulled him to the ground.